Science Magic for Kids

68 Simple & Safe Experiments

William R. Wellnitz, Ph.D.

TAB **TAB BOOKS**
Blue Ridge Summit, PA

FIRST EDITION
FIRST PRINTING

Copyright 1990 by **TAB BOOKS**
Printed in the United States of America

Library of Congress Cataloging-in-Publication Data

Wellnitz, William R., 1949-
   Science magic for kids : simple & safe experiments / by William R. Wellnitz.
     p.   cm.
   Summary: Over 60 science experiments test the properties of
colors, food, air, soap bubbles, heat, light, plants, and magnets.
   ISBN 0-8306-8423-9   ISBN 0-8306-3423-1 (pbk.)
   1. Science—Experiments—Juvenile literature. [1. Science-
-Experiments. 2. Experiments.] I. Title.
Q164.W435 1990
507.8—dc20   89-77524
                                      CIP
                                      AC

TAB BOOKS offers software for sale. For information and a catalog, please contact TAB
Software Department, Blue Ridge Summit, PA 17294-0850.

Questions regarding the content of this book should be addressed to:

   Reader Inquiry Branch
   TAB BOOKS
   Blue Ridge Summit, PA 17294-0214

Acquisitions Editor: Kimberly Tabor
Technical Editor: Lori Flaherty
Production: Katherine Brown

To Cassie, Joshua, and Shane,
for whom the experiments were initially designed.

Contents

Acknowledgments

Special thanks to Valerie Spratlin for the many excellent photographs; to two of my children, Cassie and Joshua, for serving as models and enduring three photo sessions; to my stepson, Shane Meador for most of the drawings; and to the children in my Saturday science classes for fine-tuning the experiments. A very special thanks to my wife, Dianne, for her help and support with *all* stages of this project.

Note to Children

I wrote this book for you to have fun with science. Your kitchen or yard can become your own science laboratory. You don't need fancy equipment. Almost everything you need can be found in your home.

Many of the experiments will surprise you. They might seem like magic, and you can amaze your friends with "tricks." But the experiments are not magic. They are all based on the rules of science.

Look through the book and find one or two experiments you find interesting. Each experiment tells you at the start what happens. Gather all of the materials you will need for the experiment before you begin, and keep them in one place.

Read the procedure next, but do not read the explanation until you have done the experiment. You are now ready to do the experiment. Follow the directions exactly as they are written. You can look at the pictures to see if you have set up things correctly.

Use all of your senses as you observe what happens. If you must write something down, do it as soon as you make the measurement or observation. Your memory is often not as good as it seems.

Try to figure out what happened during the experiment and why. You might want to repeat the experiment one or two more times to be sure you understand. You can then look at the explanation to see if you figured it out correctly. Try to talk about the experiment with an adult. After you have done the experiment, try changing some of the materials and experiment on your own. Be curious! Have fun!

If you have questions, or did some new and interesting things, or would just like to comment on the book, please write to me: Dr. Bill Wellnitz, Biology Department, Augusta College, Augusta, Georgia 30910.

I listen and I forget
I see and I learn
I do and I understand
—Chinese proverb

Note to Parents

This book had its origin with my children. Many times when they had friends over, rather than making cookies, we would do science experiments in the kitchen. Our kitchen became a wonderful laboratory, and soon the number of children wanting to do kitchen science exceeded the space of our kitchen. The demand for science experiments and experience quickly grew into a weekend continuing education class at Augusta College.

The intent of this book is threefold: 1) To expose children to scientific principles and procedures; 2) to show children that science is, and can be, fun; and 3) to stimulate thinking and creativity. By showing young children that science is fun, I hope to encourage them to maintain an interest in, and an appreciation for, science.

Understanding scientific concepts requires active participation, but it is not necessary to use sophisticated equipment. Stimulating creative thinking often involves exposure to a discrepant, or surprising, event. Convincing children that science is fun demands that they be allowed to play and experiment on their own. Consequently, the simple, safe experiments in this book use items that are readily available in the home, often appear as magic tricks, and are open-ended. All experiments have been "kid-tested" many times, and most require less than 30 minutes to complete.

Although most of the experiments can be done by children alone, I encourage you to become involved, but only as a guide. A few experiments demand your assistance and should not be done by children alone. These experiments require boiling liquids on a stove and are clearly indicated by a warning in boldface type. Help them find the materials, but let them do the experiment themselves. Discuss the results with them, and encourage them to think of explanations and other uses of the process involved.

Two important aspects of science are observation and measurement. Encourage your children to use all of their senses, to measure accurately, and to record their observations. For some experiments, I have provided graphs to show children how to present results.

Many of the experiments are intentionally open-ended. Children are naturally curious and will want to vary the procedure or try different materials. Don't become alarmed if they do this, just make certain they do the experiment as written on their first attempt. Many a great discovery has come from someone modifying an existing procedure.

The experiments in this book provide a solid background in scientific principles and methodology, and the techniques can easily be applied to other situations. Some of the experiments, with expansion and modification, could easily become science fair projects, but my intent is not to provide a listing of science fair projects. If your child does a science fair project, be sure that he or she actually does the work.

Many science items are readily available commercially. The gift shops of museums, and especially science museums, have excellent, high-quality, inexpensive (under $10) items that make great gifts for children and adults. Many of the museums, as well as companies, have catalogs for mail orders. One such company with excellent items is: *Edmond Scientific,* 101 E. Gloucester Pike, Barrington, NJ 08007-1380.

Finally, you might enjoy many of the experiments; and, if you have a phobia of science, you, too, might discover that science can be fun. I welcome your comments about the book, and my address appears in Note to Children.

1
Chemistry of Color

Imagine a world without color. It would seem dull. Did you know that there are companies that have large groups of scientists who do nothing but study different colors?

Many colors or dyes come from plants. Some of these dyes change colors when they are mixed with other chemicals. Other dyes are used for clothing. Other colors result from mixing different colors together.

In this chapter, you will watch dyes "mysteriously" change colors, try to obtain dyes from plants, and separate different colors.

1 MAGICAL COLOR CHANGE

Adult Supervision Required

You can easily perform magical color changes in the kitchen. A light purple solution will turn pink, blue, green, or yellow, depending on what ingredients you add to the original solution.

MATERIALS

- ☐ 5 to 10 red cabbage leaves
- ☐ small, clear bottles or glasses
- ☐ 1 cup of water
- ☐ various foods (vinegar, baking soda, apple juice, lemon juice, etc.)
- ☐ 1 teaspoon

Fig. 1-1. Two items that can be added to cabbage water.

PROCEDURE

1 Place 5 to 10 red cabbage leaves in a small pan. (Don't use green cabbage, because it won't work.) Cover the cabbage with about one cup (250ml) of water.

2 Boil the leaves for 10 minutes. Please let an adult help you with this.

3 Remove the leaves.

4 Pour 4 or 5 teaspoons (about 1 ounce or 30ml) of liquid, which should now be light purple, into several, small clear containers. Test tubes are best, but any small container such as an empty aspirin bottle, jelly jar, or glass will do fine.

5 Add a few drops or about a half teaspoon of vinegar, lemon juice, etc. to the glass. Notice how the glass changes color.

6 If you have only one glass, you can pour out the liquid and add another 4 or 5 teaspoons of purple liquid.

7 Try adding 1 or 2 pinches of baking soda to another glass. Notice how the color differs from the vinegar glass.

8 You can try all sorts of liquids, foods, or spices and determine what color the liquid becomes. Cleaning solution with ammonia will produce a new color. Liquids with deep colors, such as tomato juice, coffee, or cola, don't work

too well because their own color masks the color change. You can still try these if you use just 1 or 2 drops, however.

9 Try mixing tubes of different colors to see what color the mixture becomes. The color might not be what you expect.

EXPLANATION

The red cabbage contains a dye that boiling water removes from the leaves. The dye changes color as the solution becomes acidic, or basic. Lemon juice and vinegar are acidic; baking soda is basic.

Young children will enjoy the color changes without any explanation.

2 MAGICAL VOICES

This experiment is great fun if a group of five or more is present. Each person speaks into a bottle of liquid, and then passes the bottle to the next person. At some point, the color of the liquid will change.

MATERIALS

- ☐ 1 bottle phenol red (available in drug stores or pool supply stores)
- ☐ 1 box baking soda
- ☐ 1 cup water
- ☐ 1 clear jar with lid, the jar should hold at least 2 cups (16 ounces or ¹/₂ liter)

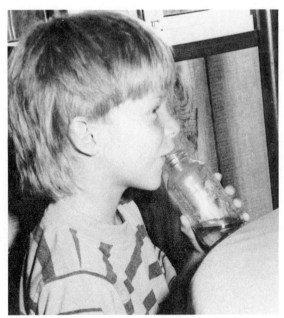

Fig. 1-2. Talking into a bottle containing phenol red.

PROCEDURE

1 Pour 1 cup of water into the jar.

2 Add 2 to 3 drops of phenol red to the water. Swirl the jar. The color should be red. If it isn't, add 1 to 2 small pinches of baking soda until the solution is light red.

3 Pass the jar from one person to another. Each person should hold the bottle close to the mouth and talk into the bottle. A good phrase is "Hocus Pocus. Make the color change now." Cover the top, then swirl the jar. Pass the bottle to the next person.

4 After a few people speak into the jar, the color will turn orange and then a bright yellow if more people talk. Keep speaking into the jar until the color changes.

If you are by yourself, you can still do this trick.

1 Do steps 1 and 2 above.

2 Blow through a straw into the liquid. Keep blowing until the color changes.

3 To make the yellow turn red again, add 1 to 2 pinches of baking soda.

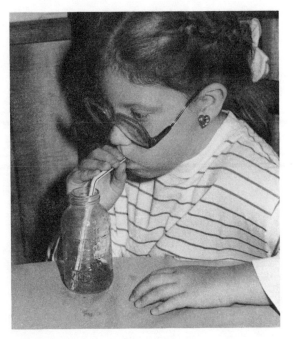

Fig. 1-3. Blowing into a bottle containing phenol red.

EXPLANATION

Phenol red is a dye that changes color under acidic or basic conditions. When someone speaks or blows, carbon dioxide is exhaled. Carbon dioxide mixes with the water and makes it acidic.

People with swimming pools use phenol red to make certain the water is safe for swimming. Adding chlorine to the water makes it acidic.

3 MAKING YOUR OWN DYES FOR EGGS OR CLOTHING

Adult Supervision Required

Many plant products contain dyes that people have used for years to dye clothes. You can use some of these dyes to make your own Easter egg colors or for dying clothing.

MATERIALS

- ☐ 1 or more eggs
- ☐ 1 teaspoon of vinegar
- ☐ 1 pan of water (about 2 cups or ¹/₂ liter)
- ☐ natural food dyes (see below)

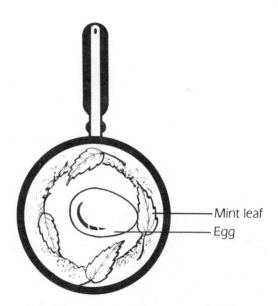

Fig. 1-4. Egg in water with mint leaves.

PROCEDURE

Simmer your eggs for twenty minutes in water, one teaspoon of vinegar, and any one of the following natural coloring agents. The more color agent used, the darker the color of the egg.

Please let an adult help you with this.

For this color:	Use this natural dye:
beige	fresh oregano or mint
blue	red cabbage leaves
brown	strong, instant coffee
buff	walnut shells
gray-gold	spinach leaves
lavender	golden delicious apple peels
orange	onion skins
yellow	orange peels or thyme

You can try the same thing with different types of white material: cotton, polyester, etc. Make the solution as directed above, except boil the cloth in the liquid for the correct amount of time. Also, you might want to experiment using baking soda instead of vinegar, but many of the colors don't seem to appear with baking soda. You might also want to experiment with other plant products. If any of them work, please write to me and let me know.

EXPLANATION

Boiling water helps pull the color out of the food. Vinegar helps the color bind to the eggs.

4 NATURAL COLORS FROM FLOWERS

Adult Supervision Required

Once you have discovered that some colors are removed by boiling water, you might want to try different colored flowers to see what removed the color. Some colors will come out in boiling water, others will come out in boiling alcohol.

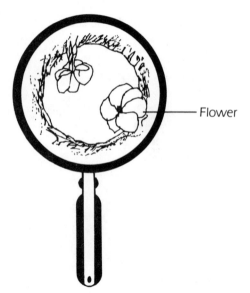

Flower

Fig. 1-5. Flowers in boiling water.

MATERIALS

- ☐ ¹/₂ to 1 cup (120 to 250ml) water
- ☐ ¹/₂ to 1 cup rubbing alcohol
- ☐ 1 small pan
- ☐ 1 electric stove or hot plate
- ☐ many different colored flowers (whatever is available)

PROCEDURE

CAUTION: BOILING ALCOHOL SHOULD BE DONE ONLY ON AN ELECTRIC STOVE OR HOT PLATE. GAS STOVES COULD CAUSE THE ALCOHOL TO BURN. THESE EXPERIMENTS MUST BE DONE WITH THE HELP OF AN ADULT.

1 Place 1 or 2 flowers in a half cup of boiling water. Boil for 10 minutes. Does the color come out of the flower?

2 If the color does not come out, add 1 or 2 teaspoons of vinegar and continue boiling. You might have to add some more water at this time.

3 If the color still does not come out, remove the flowers and water and put a half cup of rubbing alcohol in the pan and flowers. Boil for 10 minutes. Let an adult help you with this boiling. Does the color come out now?

4 Repeat this procedure with different colored flowers from different plants. Different plants with the same color might behave differently. Some plants might have a color that comes out in water. The color of other plants might come out in alcohol. You might also want to try this experiment with different berries, fruits, orange peels, etc.

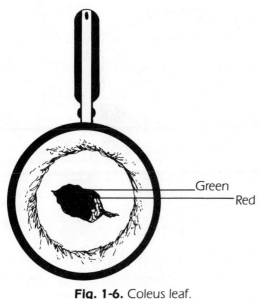

Green
Red

Fig. 1-6. Coleus leaf.

5 COLORS FROM COLEUS LEAVES

Adult Supervision Required

You can demonstrate the behavior of different colors by using Coleus leaves. This plant is available in most garden stores or florists, because it is used as a house plant or bedding plant. Many Coleus plants have green and red leaves.

MATERIALS

☐ ¹/₂ to 1 cup water
☐ ¹/₂ to 1 cup rubbing alcohol
☐ small pan
☐ Coleus leaves
☐ Electric stove or Hot plate

PROCEDURE

CAUTION: BOILING ALCOHOL SHOULD BE DONE ONLY ON AN ELECTRIC STOVE OR HOT PLATE. GAS STOVES COULD CAUSE THE ALCOHOL TO BURN. THESE EXPERIMENTS MUST BE DONE WITH THE HELP OF AN ADULT.

1 Boil the leaf in water for 10 minutes. Which color is removed from the leaf ?

2 Remove the leaf, pour out the water, and add rubbing alcohol to the pan.

3 Boil again. What happens this time?
   What can you say about the red pigment? What can you say about the green pigment?

EXPLANATION

Some colors or chemicals dissolve in water. Other chemicals dissolve in alcohol. This experiment shows that not all colors dissolve in water. The dyes that are used to color clothes usually do not dissolve in water. What would happen to your clothes if the colors did dissolve in water?

6 SEPARATING COLORS ON STRIPS OF PAPER

This experiment allows you to separate different colors and to make some pretty, abstract designs.

MATERIALS

- ☐ strips of paper cut from coffee filters
- ☐ 1 pencil
- ☐ 1 paper clip or bobby pin
- ☐ 1 piece of thread, about 3 inches (7 to 8cm)
- ☐ 1 metal tie from bread package
- ☐ 1 jar, about one quart (1 liter)
- ☐ colored marking pens and/or food colorings
- ☐ water

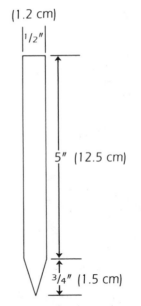

(1.2 cm)

1/2"

5" (12.5 cm)

3/4" (1.5 cm)

Fig. 1-7. Shape of strips to be used.

PROCEDURE

1 Cut out a few strips of paper (from the coffee filters), about the same size shown in Fig. 1-7.

2 Cut a few more strips the same shape, but two inches (5cm) wide.

3 With a pencil, draw a light line on the strip about 3/4 inch (15mm) from the tip.

4 If you have colored markers, place a dot on the center of the line. Be sure to try black or green at some time. If you have food colorings, mix a drop of food coloring with 1 tablespoon of water. With a paint brush or toothpick, put 1 to 2 drops in one place on the line.

5 Attach the strip of paper to the paper clip or bobby pin as shown in Fig. 1-8. Tie one end of the thread around the center of the pencil and the other end to the paper clip or bobby pin.

6 Pour just enough water in the jar to cover the bottom of the jar.

7 Position the pencil over the top of the jar so that the strip is suspended inside the jar. Adjust the strip so that just the tip of the strip touches the water. Be careful not to let water cover the drop of color.

8 Wait 5 to 15 minutes and watch the colors separate. Remove the strip.

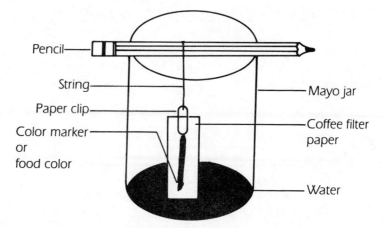

Pencil

String

Paper clip

Color marker
or
food color

Mayo jar

Coffee filter
paper

Water

Fig. 1-8. Setup for color separation.

You can also do this experiment with the wider strips. Place different colors at different spaces along the line and repeat steps 5 through 8. In this way, you can have a race to see which colors move faster. Other colored solutions, such as Kool-aid and fruit juices, can also be used. With a toothpick or small paint brush, put 4 to 8 drops in one place on the paper and repeat steps 5 through 8.

EXPLANATION

The procedure used here is called paper chromotography. Colors move up the paper at different rates because they mix unevenly with water. Scientists often use this procedure to isolate or separate different chemicals. You will probably be surprised to see the different colors that make up the original color. For a similar experiment, see Experiment 7.

7 SEPARATING COLORS TO MAKE PICTURES

This experiment works the same way as Experiment 6, but it produces a nice multicolored picture.

MATERIALS

☐ 1 coffee filter
☐ 1 baking pan or cookie tray, with
    1/4 inch (5mm) water on the bottom
☐ colored marking pens and/or food colorings

Fig. 1-9. Paper chromotography with a coffee filter.

PROCEDURE

1 Place many dots of many different colors about 3/4 inch (15mm) from the edge of the filter. Do this all around the edges of the paper.

2 Fold the coffee filter in half as shown in Fig. 1-9.

3 Place the paper in water. Do not let the water cover the dots. Also, be careful not to let the filter fall over into the water. Watch the colors move.

4 Remove the paper from the water and allow it to dry. You now have used a scientific procedure to make a picture.

5 You might want to try a different method. Instead of putting dots in one place, place different colored dots all over the filter. As the lower color meets a different color, a new color might form.

Newspaper and paper towels do not work well for this experiment. You might want to try white construction paper, or if you made paper in experiment 68, you might want to try this experiment on that paper. You can also use the same procedure to make colored chalk, but the colors take much longer to separate. To do this, draw a colored ring around the white chalk about 3/4 inch (15mm) from the bottom. Place the chalk in a small amount of water and wailt (30-40 minutes at least).

EXPLANATION

The procedure used here is called paper chromotography. Colors move up the paper at different rates because they mix unevenly with water. Scientists often use this procedure to isolate or separate different chemicals. You will probably be surprised to see the different colors that make up the original color.

2

Properties of Air

Air is all around us, but many times we are unaware of what air can do. Air pushes on all things and can be used to break things. Moving air can be used to move objects in strange, unexpected ways.

Air takes up space. As air is heated, it expands or takes up more space, and sometimes causes things to move or to change. Other properties of air allow you to make paper "airplanes" without wings. In this chapter you will see how air can break a piece of wood and how air that is moving moves objects.

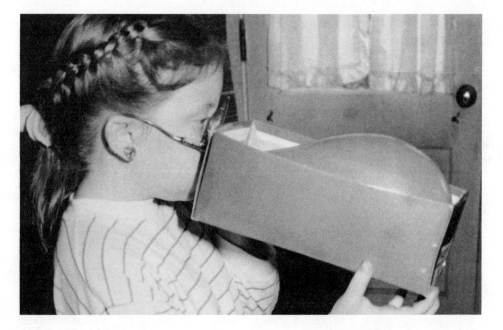

8 BREAKING A STICK WITH NEWSPAPER

When you cover a piece of wood, such as a yardstick, with newspaper and hit the wood, the wood breaks. Most people expect the newspaper to fly into the air.

MATERIALS

☐ 1 piece of plywood or paneling, $1/8$ to $1/4$ inch (2 to 5mm) thick, 1 to 2 inches (2 to 5cm) wide, and 18 to 24 inches (50 to 75cm) long
☐ 1 to 3 sheets of newspaper
☐ 1 cup of water (optional)

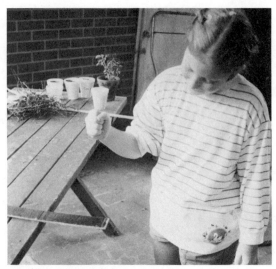

Fig. 2-1. Hitting the wood on a table.

PROCEDURE

1 Place the wood on the table so that about 6 to 10 inches (15 to 25cm) of it hangs over the edge.

2 Hit the wood hard with your fist. The wood should fall off the table.

3 Return the wood to the table as directed in step 1.

4 Open a sheet of newspaper and place it over the wood. The edge of the paper should touch the edge of the table.

5 Smooth out the newspaper so that it is flat against the table.

6 Place 1 to 2 more sheets of newspaper on top of the first sheet, and smooth out the paper. There should be little, if any, air under the paper.

7 Hit the edge of the wood hard with your hand. The stick should break.

8 If the stick doesn't break, try sprinkling some water on the paper, then smooth it out. This procedure will help to remove air and to make a tighter seal. Then try hitting the wood again.

Fig. 2-2. Wood covered with newspaper.

EXPLANATION

Air pushes on all objects. Without the newspaper, the air is pushing down only on the wood. When you cover the wood with newspaper, the air then pushes down on the area of the newspaper. Smoothing out the newspaper removes the air from under the paper. The amount of air now pushing on the newspaper is about the same as having a car sitting on the wood.

9 KEEPING PAPER DRY UNDER WATER

Show a friend that you can keep paper dry under water.

MATERIALS

☐ 1 drinking glass or cup
☐ 1 piece of paper, crumbled into a ball
☐ sinkful of water

Fig. 2-3. How to keep paper dry.

PROCEDURE

1 Fill the sink with water.
2 Place the crumbled paper into the bottom of the glass.
3 Hold the glass upside down and straight up and down.
4 Quickly push the glass into the water.
5 Pull the glass straight up and remove paper. Is it dry?

EXPLANATION

Air takes up space. In the glass, air surrounded the paper. When you push the glass straight down into the water, the air stays in the glass. Water can not enter the glass. If you tilt the glass, air can escape, and water can enter. The paper will get wet.

Fig. 2-4. A race with straws.

10 THE "MAGIC" STRAW

In this experiment, you and your friend race to see who can empty a glass faster with a straw. You will always win.

MATERIALS

☐ 2 glasses, full with liquid
☐ 2 straws, ones with colored stripes are best
☐ 1 pin

PROCEDURE

1 Before your friend arrives, use a pin to punch many small holes in one straw. Try to punch the holes in the stripes so the holes can't be seen.

2 Tell your friend you can suck up the liquid faster than he can.

3 Each person takes a straw and begins to suck the liquid.

4 Be sure to give your friend the straw with the holes.

5 Your friend will not be able to suck up much liquid.

EXPLANATION

Air pushes on all things. In a regular straw, no air can enter. The air pushes down on the liquid and forces it up the straw. In the straw with holes, air rushes into the holes and pushes down on the liquid, so it doesn't move up as quickly.

11 LIFTING PAPER BY BLOWING

When you blow above a strip of paper, it magically rises.

MATERIALS

☐ 1 strip of paper, about 1 inch (2 to 3cm) wide and 6 to 8 inches (15 to 20cm) long

Fig. 2-5. Blowing above a strip of paper.

PROCEDURE

1 Grasp one end of the paper between thumb and finger.

2 Hold the paper just under the edge of your lower lip.

3 Blow straight out and watch the paper rise.
   This experiment takes a little practice. You might have to move the paper around some to find the correct position.

EXPLANATION

As you saw in Experiment 9, air pushes on all things. Air that is moving pushes less than air that is not moving. It is as if moving air is removed from the space. When you blew over the paper, the air above the paper was moving. The air pushing under the paper was not moving, and therefore, pushed stronger on the paper, making it rise.

The effect of moving air is called Bernouilli's principle. This principle helps airplanes to rise off the ground. Air moves more slowly under the wing and pushes the plane up. Tennis players use the same principle when they put spin on the ball. The next two experiments also deal with Bernouilli's principle.

Fig. 2-6. Blowing under an index card.

12 THE FLATTENED INDEX CARD

By blowing *under* a bent index card, you can make it flat.

MATERIALS

☐ 1 index card

PROCEDURE

1 Fold the card in half.
2 Open the card and place it on a table near the edge.
3 Place your mouth even with the table and blow under the card.
4 Watch what happens to the card.
  This experiment, like Experiment 11, might require a little practice to set the correct position.

EXPLANATION

Moving air pushes less than static air. The air above the card is not moving and pushes down on the card. When you blew under the card, the air below it was moving. The air above the card was pushing stronger on the card, causing it to flatten.

13 COLLIDING BALLS

This experiment will surprise you. Two balls will collide when you expect them to move apart.

MATERIALS

☐ Enough books to make two stacks about 6 to 8 inches (15 to 20cm) high. Alternatively, any objects that stack 6 to 8 inches high.
☐ Tape
☐ 1 board or stick, about 20 inches (50cm) long
☐ 2 pieces of string, each about 6 inches (15cm) long
☐ 2 balls—ping pong or nerf balls are best, but other balls also work. Apples or lemons work too.
☐ 1 ruler

Fig. 2-7. Making balls collide.

PROCEDURE

1 Tape the string to each ball.

2 Set up the books and ruler as shown in Fig. 2-7.

3 Tie one end of the string to the stick so that the balls are about 1 inch (2 to 3cm) apart. Then tape the other ends to the balls. Be sure balls can swing freely without touching the table top.

4 You are going to blow between the two balls. What do you think will happen? Will they move apart or collide?

5 Place your mouth so you can blow straight between the balls and blow. This might take some practice to find the proper position.

6 What happens to the balls?

7 Now move one of the strings so that the balls are about 1¹/₂ inches (about 4cm) apart, then blow again.

8 Do the balls still move?

9 Repeat steps 7 and 8, making the balls ¹/₂ (1cm) farther apart each time.

10 Keep moving the balls apart until they no longer move.

EXPLANATION

The air on the outside of the balls is not moving, but the air between the balls is moving. Remember, moving air pushes less. By changing the distance between the balls, you determined how far moving air can work. When scientists test something, they usually test it under different situations like you did.

14 INFLATING A BALLOON WITHOUT BLOWING INTO IT

In this experiment, you can again act like a magician. A balloon will inflate or deflate depending on where you place it. You can reverse this process many times by putting a bottle in pans of water that are different temperatures. The behavior of the balloon makes the water seem to have magical properties. Actually, you are observing a property of air.

MATERIALS

☐ 1 small narrow-mouth bottle—a disposable soft drink bottle works well
☐ 1 balloon
☐ 1 pan of cold water
☐ 1 pan of hot water

Fig. 2-8. A balloon on a jar in cold water.

PROCEDURE

1 Place the end of the balloon over the top of the bottle. Make sure the balloon is secure and completely covers the top of the bottle. The balloon should hang on the side of the bottle as shown in Fig. 2-8.

2 Place the balloon in cold water for five minutes. You might want to add a few ice cubes, but this is not necessary.

3 Now place the bottle in warm or hot water. Watch what happens to the balloon.

4 Return the bottle to the cold water. What happens to the balloon now?

5 You can repeat steps 2 and 3 many times.

Fig. 2-9. The balloon on the jar in hot water "magically" inflates.

EXPLANATION

As air warms, it expands. Placing the bottle in hot water warms the air in the bottle. The only place for the air to go is into the balloon. Placing the balloon in cold water causes the volume (the space occupied by air) to shrink. The air leaves the balloon and the balloon shrinks.

You can use this same idea to make non-bouncy tennis balls bounce again. Wrap the balls in aluminum foil and place in a 200°F (90°C) for 10 to 15 minutes. The air in the balls will expand, and the balls will bounce well for about two hours.

15 THE DANCING COIN

You can make a coin move up and down on top of a bottle.

MATERIALS

☐ 1 small glass, soft drink bottle
☐ 1 coin
☐ water from the faucet

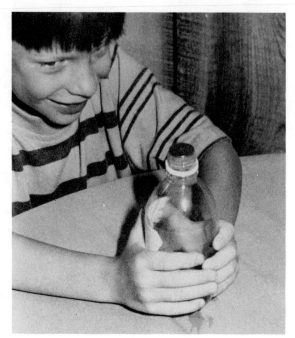

Fig. 2-10. Coin on top of bottle.

PROCEDURE

1 Wet your hand and moisten the top of the bottle.

2 Wet one side of the coin.

3 Place the coin on the top of the bottle with the wet side touching the bottle.

4 Hold the bottle in your hands or place the bottle in a sink of hot water.

5 Watch what happens to the coin.

EXPLANATION

This experiment works similar to Experiment 14. Warm air rises and expands. The heat from your hand causes the air inside the bottle to expand and to push on the coin.

Fig. 2-11. Can in boiling water.

16 THE SHRINKING CAN

Adult Supervision Required

A metal can sitting on the table suddenly collapses.

MATERIALS

☐ 1 rectangular metal can with a screw-cap lid. A can from paint thinner works well.
☐ ¹/₄ cup or 2 ozs. of water
☐ stove or hot plate
☐ 1 frying pan

PROCEDURE

CAUTION: MAKE SURE THE CAN HAS BEEN RINSED THOROUGHLY. THE HEATING STEP SHOULD BE DONE BY AN ADULT.

1 Rinse the empty can 5 to 10 times with water until you are sure it is clean.

2 Place the water in the can, and tighten the lid.

3 The can will balance better on the burner or stove if you place it in a frying pan. Add a little water to the bottom of the frying pan, about ¹/₄ inch. Let an adult help you with this.

4 Heat the can about 5 minutes.

5 Remove the can from the heat and allow it to cool.

6 After 5 to 10 minutes, the can will crumble. If it doesn't, place the can in a sink of cold water.

EXPLANATION

Air pushes on all things. Air also expands when it is heated. When you heated the can, the water boiled and turned to steam or gas. As the can cooled, the steam again became water. At this point, air outside the can pushed more on the can than air inside the can.

17 MAKING A BALLOON TOY

You can use a balloon to provide power to move something.

MATERIALS

- ☐ 1 empty shoe box
- ☐ 1 balloon
- ☐ 1 pencil
- ☐ many straws, crayons, or marking pens

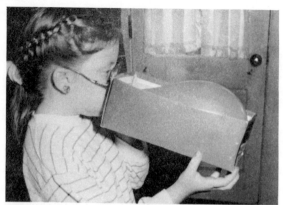

Fig. 2-12. Blowing up a balloon.

PROCEDURE

1 Place many straws or other round objects on the floor, about 3 to 4 inches (7 to 10cm) apart.

2 With a pencil, punch a hole in one end of the shoe box.

3 Blow up the balloon. Hold the end of the balloon while you put it in the box. Push the end of the balloon through the hole, being careful to hold the end. The blown balloon should be large enough to fill the box. If you find this difficult, you can put the balloon through the hole and then blow it up.

4 Hold the end of the balloon and place the other end of the box on the straws.

5 Release the balloon and watch the box move.

Fig. 2-13. Racing a balloon toy.

EXPLANATION

For every force that pushes in one direction, there is an equal force that pushes in the opposite direction. The famous physicist, Isaac Newton, discovered this fact over 300 years ago. As air leaves the balloon, another force pushes the box along the straws. This principle is used in airplanes and in nature by clams. The straws make it easier for the box to move by causing less friction.

You can have races with two boxes and two sets of straws, or you can see which box will travel farther.

18 SUCKING WATER INTO A JAR

Adult Supervision Required

Water magically enters an upside down jar.

MATERIALS

- ☐ 1 short, fat candle, about 1 to 2 inches (2 to 5cm) high and 1 to 2 inches (2 to 5cm) in diameter.
- ☐ 1 plate
- ☐ 1 large-mouth jar. A large mayonnaise jar works well
- ☐ ¹/₂ to 1 cup water (4 to 8 ounces or 100 to 250ml)

Fig. 2-14. Place the jar over the candle.

PROCEDURE

CAUTION: HAVE AN ADULT LIGHT THE CANDLE FOR YOU.

1 Place the plate on the counter.

2 Pour water into the plate so that the whole plate is covered with water.

3 Place the candle in the middle of the plate.

4 Place the jar over the candle. Does anything happen to the water?

5 Remove the jar, and have an adult light the candle for you. Immediately place the jar over the burning candle. What happens to the water now?

6 Hold the plate over the sink when you remove the jar. If you do not do this, then the water will spill over the counter.

Fig. 2-15. Placing the jar over the burning candle.

EXPLANATION

When anything burns, some oxygen is used up. After the candle burns, there is less air in the jar, and therefore less pressure. The air outside pushes the water into the jar. Steps 4 and 5 show that the process requires burning and not just the jar.

19 THE POWERFUL BALLOON

You can pick up two cups with a balloon and suspend them in air.

MATERIALS

☐ 1 round balloon
☐ 2 plastic or styrofoam cups, about the same size

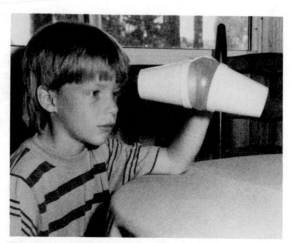

Fig. 2-16. Holding cups with a balloon.

PROCEDURE

1 Place the balloon over the edge of one cup so that the mouth part hangs over the edge of the cup.
2 Place the second cup on top of the first cup.
3 Hold the two cups and blow up the balloon.
4 Squeeze the end of the balloon to keep it inflated.
5 The cups will stay attached to the balloon.

EXPLANATION

As the balloon expands, it pushes against the cups and removes the air. Where the balloon and cups meet, a vacuum is created and the two cups stick to the balloon. Suction cups that hook things to walls work the same way. If you tightly tie the end of the balloon, you can hang the balloon and the cups from a string to make an interesting mobile.

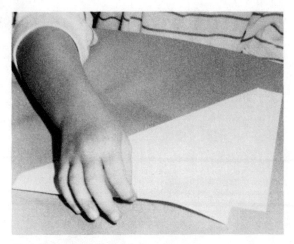

Fig. 2-17. The first fold.

20 A PAPER AIRPLANE WITHOUT WINGS

You can make a paper "airplane" that can fly a long distance without wings.

MATERIALS

☐ 1 piece of notebook paper

PROCEDURE

1 Fold a piece of paper to make a triangle with overlapping edges. See Fig. 2-17.

2 Fold the fold over itself 2 times. See Fig. 2-18.

3 Push one end of the folded side into the other end. When your finished, the "airplane" should look like a crown. See Fig. 2-19.

4 Hold the top of the "crown" between your first two fingers.

5 Gently toss the plane and watch it glide. See Fig. 2-20.

This design is similar to the design of the space shuttle.

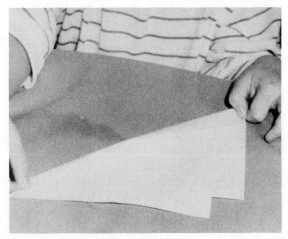

Fig. 2-18. The second fold.

Fig. 2-19. Joining the ends.

Fig. 2-20. Throwing the wingless airplane.

EXPLANATION

Air moves easily around curved structures. If air moves easily, there is less friction, or resistance, on the object. The object moves easier through the air. This design is similar to the design of the space shuttle.

3

Food and Nutrition

Different types of foods are great items to use in experiments. Different foods contain different kinds of molecules: fats, starches, and protein. It is simple to see which foods contain fat or starch.

Food also provides nourishment for small forms of life such as bacteria and molds. As these microbes grow, they often change the food and sometimes make it spoil. In this chapter, you will learn about the different properties of food.

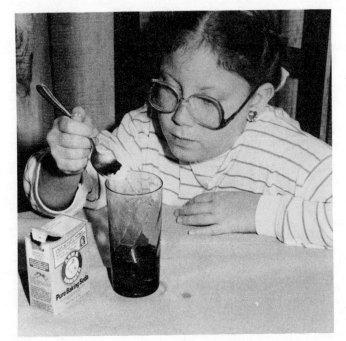

21 DETECTING STARCH IN FOOD

Many different foods contain starch. In this experiment, you will determine which foods contain starch.

Fig. 3-1. Testing bread for starch.

MATERIALS

☐ small pieces of different foods (bread, meat, cookies, etc.)
☐ Tincture of iodine (an antiseptic, available in drug stores)

PROCEDURE

1 Place a couple of drops of iodine on the piece of food.
2 Look for a blue-black color. If you see blue-black, the food has starch.
3 Try to test many different kinds of foods for starch and make a list of those that have starch.

EXPLANATION

Iodine reacts with starch to form a dark blue or black color. If no starch is present, the iodine stays brown.

Fig. 3-2. Testing for fat.

22 DETECTING FAT OR GREASE IN FOODS

Lots of different foods contain fat. In this experiment you will determine which foods contain fat.

MATERIALS

☐ small pieces of many different foods (candy bar, bread, butter, meat etc.)
☐ small pieces of paper—1 for each piece of food. A cut up paper grocery bag works well

PROCEDURE

1 Take a small piece of butter.
2 Place butter or other food on paper for 5 minutes.
3 Remove food and examine paper. If the food left a shiny spot on the paper, the food has fat in it.
4 Try many different foods and make a list of those that have fat.

EXPLANATION

A little bit of fat leaves the food and makes a greasy spot on the paper. You can easily see the difference the grease makes on the paper.

23 PLAYING DETECTIVE WITH EGGS

Imagine that you are a detective and you have to tell if an egg in the refrigerator has been cooked. This experiment shows you how to do this.

MATERIALS

☐ 1 hard boiled egg (have an adult help you make this)
☐ 1 uncooked egg

Fig. 3-3. Spinning an egg.

PROCEDURE

1 Hold one of the eggs upright on the counter. Be sure the large end of the egg is down toward the counter.
2 Try to spin the egg.
3 If the egg spins, it is cooked. If the egg immediately falls over, it is not cooked.

EXPLANATION

In a cooked egg, all of the insides are solid, and do not move around. The inside of a raw egg is liquid, and sloshes around. When you try to spin a raw egg, the liquid moves, and the egg immediately falls over.

Fig. 3-4. Popcorn soaking in water.

24 POPPING ALL OF THE POPCORN KERNELS

When you make popcorn, some of the kernels fail to pop. This experiment shows you how to get all of them to pop.

MATERIALS

☐ unpopped kernels from popped corn
☐ 1 small jar
☐ ¹/₂ cup (4 ounces or 100ml) water
☐ popcorn popper

PROCEDURE

1 Place the "dud" kernels—those that did not pop—in jar.
2 Cover the kernels with the water.
3 Let the kernels soak 5 to 10 minutes and remove.
4 They now should pop.

EXPLANATION

Popcorn pops because of a little bit of water in the kernels. As the water heats up, it turns to steam or gas. The gas, like air, pushes on the sides of the kernels until the kernel pops and the steam escapes.

Companies that say all of their kernels pop use this idea. All of the kernels are soaked in water and then placed in tight jars. When the water leaves the kernels, or evaporates, it stays in the jar and is eventually pushed back into the kernels. Storing popcorn in a jar is better than storing it in a bag.

25 THE FLOATING SOFT DRINK CAN

Some full soft drinks will sink when placed in water. Other drinks will float.

MATERIALS

- ☐ 1 unopened can of regular soft drink
- ☐ 1 unopened can of diet soft drink, preferably one with Nutrasweet
- ☐ 1 large bucket or sink
- ☐ water to fill the bucket or sink

Fig. 3-5. Soft drink cans in water.

PROCEDURE

1 Fill the bucket with water.

2 Place the regular can in the water. What happens?

3 Place the diet can in the water. What happens?

EXPLANATION

The liquid in the regular can weighs much more than the liquid in a diet drink. Regular soft drinks contain a large amount of sugar to make them sweet. Diet soft drinks contain a very small amount of Nutrasweet or other artificial sugar. For this reason, the regular can will always sink and the diet can will always float.

Fig. 3-6. Placing food and water into bags.

26 ISOLATING MICROBES FROM AIR

The air is full of many small organisms that are too small to see with the naked eye. These organisms are called microbes. Some of them are bacteria and others are molds or fungi. Scientists use agar, a seaweed product that is like gelatin, to grow microbes. The microbes grow until you can see them. You can use different types of foods to do the same thing. This experiment takes two to five days to complete.

MATERIALS

- ☐ 1 piece of cheese, about 1 inch (2 to 3cm) square
- ☐ 1 piece of bread
- ☐ 1 potato chip
- ☐ 1 slice of apple
- ☐ 1 small piece of lunch meat
- ☐ plastic sandwich bags (optional)
- ☐ 1 cookie sheet or plate

PROCEDURE

1 Place various pieces of food on the cookie sheet or plate.

2 Place the cookie sheet where it won't be disturbed, or thrown out by parents. The top of a desk, chest, or table will all work.

3 Examine the food each day for 7 to 10 days.

4 Record what, if anything grows on each food. Try to describe the microbe as much as possible.

5 If you have a magnifying glass, look at the growth with the magnifying glass.

ALTERNATIVE PROCEDURE

1 Place several pieces of food on the counter for 30 to 45 minutes, then place them in a plastic zip-lock sandwich bag.

2 Add 1 to 2 tablespoons of water to the bag.

3 Seal the bag.

4 Place all of the bags where they will be warm as in step 2 of part one.

5 Examine the foods each day.

Did all of the foods grow microbes? Were all the microbes the same?

EXPLANATION

Lots of microbes can be found in the air. When they fall onto food, they begin to grow. Some microbes grow best on starchy food, such as bread, potatoes, etc. Other microbes grow better on foods with protein, such as cheese and meat. Some foods will not allow microbes to grow. You might not have seen any growth on the food in some of the bags. The food probably was not exposed to air long enough. You can try many different types of foods if your parents will allow you. Keep a record of what foods grow microbes and how quickly the microbes appear. Also, try many different types of bread.

Foods kept in the refrigerator usually don't show molds. The cold temperature makes the microbes grow very slowly. You don't see them unless you wait a long time.

Fig. 3-7. Chocolate and whole milk in jars.

27 CHANGES IN MILK OVER TIME

Milk provides a wonderful environment for many different small organisms to grow. As the organisms grow, they produce many changes in the milk. Sometimes the milk begins to get solid, or curdle. Other times, it begins to take on foul smelling odors. You can do this by yourself, but it works better if two or three people do this experiment together. You will need to look at the milk every day for at least one week.

MATERIALS

- ☐ ¹/₂ cup (4 ounces or 100ml) of at least two of the following kinds of milk: skim milk, powdered milk, chocolate milk, or boxed, long-life milk
- ☐ ¹/₂ cup of whole milk.
- ☐ ¹/₂ cup whole milk that has been boiled for 10 to 15 min.
- ☐ 2 to 6 small bottles with tops. Clean jelly jars or baby food jars work well
- ☐ 1 teaspoon
- ☐ tape
- ☐ small strips of paper for labels
- ☐ 1 pencil or pen

PROCEDURE

CAUTION: DO NOT ATTEMPT TO DRINK THE MILK THAT HAS BEEN SET OUT ON THE COUNTER AFTER THIS EXPERIMENT.

1 Wash the jars with dish detergent and rinse thoroughly.

2 Ask an adult to boil ¹/₂ cup of milk for you. Let the milk boil for about 10 minutes. Allow the milk to cool.

3 Place about 8 teaspoons of the boiled milk in a jar and cover the jar. Label this jar "boiled."

4 Place about 8 teaspoons of whole milk into one jar. Cover the jar and label this jar "whole milk."

5 Place about 8 teaspoons of at least one other kind of milk into a different jar. Cover the jar and label what kind of milk you used. Do this step for the many different types of milk you use.

6 Put all of the jars on a table or counter and let them sit in the room.

7 Place 8 teaspoons of refrigerated milk in another jar. Cover the jar and label "refrigerator." Place this jar in this refrigerator.

8 Look at each jar each day and describe what the milk looks like. Has it begun to get solid? Has it begun to smell? How does it smell? Write down what you see and smell each day.

9 Do step 8 every day for at least a week.

EXPLANATION

Most types of milk contain many different types of bacteria. Some of these bacteria are used to make yogurt and cheese. As the bacteria in the milk begins to grow, it begins to change the nature of the milk. Different types of milk have different amounts and types of bacteria in them, and produce different results. Milk that has been left on the counter for a few days, or even a few hours, is not safe to drink.

Which type of milk became solid the quickest? Why do you think this happened? What happened to the milk that you kept in the refrigerator? Why do you think we put many different foods in the fridge? Hint: organisms grow more slowly at cool temperatures.

What happened to the milk that had been boiled? Did it change like the milk that had not been boiled? Most forms of life can not survive very high temperatures, like those that were boiled. When you boiled the milk, you killed almost everything living in the milk. When milk is taken from a cow, it is quickly heated to a high temperature. The high temperature kills the bacteria that can make you sick.

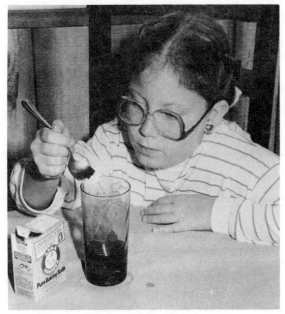

28 MAKING VINEGAR FROM APPLE JUICE

Some companies use apple juice to make vinegar. You can do the same thing at home, but you must be patient. This experiment takes many days.

MATERIALS

- ☐ 1 cup (8 ounces or 250ml) of apple juice
- ☐ 1 small jar or drinking glass
- ☐ 1 box baking soda

Fig. 3-8. Testing apple juice for vinegar.

PROCEDURE

1 Pour the apple juice into a glass or jar. Do not cover the jar.
2 Place the apple juice on the counter.
3 Each day test the apple juice for vinegar. To do this, remove 2 to 3 teaspoons of apple juice. Put this removed juice in a small glass. Add a pinch of baking soda to the new glass. If it foams or bubbles when you add baking soda, vinegar is present.
4 Repeat step 3 until you see foam.

EXPLANATION

Some small microbes can make the sugar in apple juice into vinegar. As the microbes grow, they slowly make vinegar. Vinegar and baking soda react to form bubbles of carbon dioxide, the foam you see. For another experiment with vinegar and baking soda, see Experiment 67.

4

Soap Bubbles

Soap bubbles are some of my favorite science experiments. Did you know you can make giant bubbles and different three-dimensional shaped bubbles? You can even stick a straw through a soap bubble without the bubble breaking. Many of the experiments in this chapter are best done outside, so you can watch the bubbles travel long distances. As you will see, you can use almost any object with a hole to make bubbles.

For these experiments, you will need to make a bubble mix. Most dish detergents will work but for some reason Joy and Dawn brands seem to work best. You might want to have an adult measure for you.

To make good soap bubbles use: 1 part dish detergent (for example 3 to 4 teaspoons or 25ml) and 12 parts water (for example 1¹/₂ cups or 300ml). Mix the detergent and water gently. Try not to make too many bubbles while stirring. Mixtures with very few bubbles will probably work best. You might find that 1 part detergent and 10 parts water, or 1 part detergent and 14 parts water will work better sometimes. As the mixture begins to disappear, add some more water.

29 MAKING DOUBLE AND TRIPLE BUBBLES

Objects that you usually throw out make great double-bubble makers.

MATERIALS

- ☐ 1 plastic, six-ring holder from soft drinks
- ☐ 1 plastic strawberry container
- ☐ other thin objects with more than one hole
- ☐ detergent mix (see Chapter 4 introduction)
- ☐ 1 shallow baking dish or cookie sheet or, if inside, the sink or a frying pan

Fig. 4-1. Plastic rings for double bubbles.

PROCEDURE

1 Prepare the soap mix and pour it into a container or the sink. Less than 1 inch (2 to 3cm) of mix is best.

2 Place the six-ring holder in the mix and then remove it.

3 Slowly pull the rings through the air. You might have to try several times to get the proper speed.

4 Watch the double bubbles. With luck, you might be able to make four to six big bubbles hooked together. If you use the strawberry container, you might have to blow the bubbles out.

EXPLANATION

Molecules in the detergent mix are attracted to each other. Without the frame, the bubbles hook together. You can use any object that has more than one hole to make multiple bubbles.

30 MAKING GIANT BUBBLES

You can make giant (1 to 2 foot or 30 to 50cm) bubbles that look like ghosts. With practice, you can put yourself or friend inside a giant bubble.

MATERIALS

☐ Soap bubble mix (see Chapter 4 introduction)
☐ 1 coat hanger
☐ 1 piece of string, 2 to 3 feet (60 to 100cm) long
☐ 1 large frying pan, big bowl, or metal tub. The bowl or tub must be big enough to put a coat hanger in.

Fig. 4-2. Making a giant bubble.

PROCEDURE

1 Pour the soap mix into the pan or bowl.
2 Shape the coat hanger into a circle. The hanger will work better if you wrap string around the coat hanger.
3 Dip the hanger into the mix and slowly pull it out. Watch the huge bubble form.
4 If you like, pull the forming bubble over your friend.

You can also use just the string if you don't want to bend the coat hanger.

1 Tie the two ends of the string together.
2 Dip the string into the soap mix.
3 Spread the string apart and pull it through the air. If it is windy, just pull the string apart, and the wind will blow the bubble out of the string.

As you pull the bubble out of the mix, it looks like a ghost.

EXPLANATION

The size bubble you make depends only on what you use to make the bubble.

Fig. 4-3. Shape of homemade bubble horn.

31 BLOWING GIANT SOAP BUBBLES

You can easily make a "horn" device that will allow you to blow giant (over 6" or 15cm) bubbles. You can use items that are usually thrown out.

MATERIALS

☐ Soap bubble mix (see Chapter 4 introduction)
☐ shallow pan or cookie sheet
☐ 1 plastic soft drink bottle

PROCEDURE

1 Have an adult help you cut the soft drink bottle into the shape shown in Fig. 4-3.

2 Pour the soap mix into the pan or cookie sheet so that you have about ¹/₂" (1cm) of mix.

3 Place your "horn" into the mix and remove.

4 Gently blow into the "horn" to make a giant bubble.

5 To release the bubble, turn the "horn" and pull up.

Fig. 4-4. Using the horn to blow a bubble.

EXPLANATION

As you blow into the horn, your breath is trapped in the film of the bubble.
This device allows you to reuse something you usually throw out.

Fig. 4-5. Cube made from pipe cleaners.

32 UNUSUAL, THREE-DIMENSIONAL BUBBLES

When you dip a three-dimensional shape, such as a cube, into the soap mix, a small cube-shaped bubble forms in the middle.

MATERIALS

- ☐ soap mix (see Chapter 4 introduction)
- ☐ many pipe cleaners (If you don't have pipe cleaners, you can use toothpicks and small pieces of clay. Wire also works.)

PROCEDURE

1. Bend the pipe cleaners and hook them together to form many shapes. See Fig. 4-5. If you don't have pipe cleaners, try making the shapes with wire or toothpicks. Place a small amount of clay (about the size of half of a pencil eraser) on the ends of the toothpicks. Use the clay to hook the toothpicks together.
2. Pour the soap mix into the sink or a deep pan. The mix must be at least 4 inches (10cm) deep.
3. Hold one corner of the cube. Dip it into the soap so the soap covers the cube.
4. Pull the cube out of the mix.
5. Hold the cube in the air 10 to 20 seconds. At first, the soap will form walls on the cube. Then magically, a small cube will appear in the middle of the cube.
6. After you see the small cube, move the pipe cleaners through the air. A sphere shaped bubble will be released.

Fig. 4-6. A cube inside a cube.

EXPLANATION

As the cube sits in the air, some of the water evaporates and leaves the mix. The soap film is pulled toward the center, but it is still attached to the pipe cleaner. When the edges of the film meet, they form a shape just like the original.

Bubbles formed from any shape will always make a sphere in the air. Without walls to support the soap, it falls into a shape that needs no support, a sphere.

You will enjoy doing this experiment with many different shapes. Try making unusual shapes to see what happens.

33 Punching Holes in Bubbles

When you stick something through a bubble, many times it will not break. Instead, it will heal itself.

MATERIALS

- ☐ soap mix (see Chapter 4 introduction)
- ☐ many pipe cleaners, a string, or other items for making bubbles (plastic six-pack rings)
- ☐ shallow pan or cookie sheet
- ☐ 1 straw, toothpick, or pencil

Fig. 4-7. Punching a hole in a bubble.

PROCEDURE

1 Make a shape, such as a square or triangle with pipe cleaners.

2 Fill the shallow pan with soap mix.

3 Hold the edges of the shape and dip it into the soap mix. You should see the soap mix inside your shape.

4 Push the straw or toothpick through the soap and pull it out. You may be surprised that the soap did not break or pop. You can even stick your finger through the film if you used pipe cleaners.

5 Move the shape through the air to release a round bubble.

EXPLANATION

The chemicals in the soap mix are attracted to each other. When you remove the straw, the chemicals rush to get back together. As you learned in Experiment 32, bubbles in the air are always round.

34 BLOWING BUBBLES INSIDE OF OTHER BUBBLES

With a little practice, you can blow one bubble inside another bubble.

MATERIALS

☐ soap mix (see Chapter 4 introduction)
☐ homemade bubble horn (see Experiment 31) or three-dimensional shape from Experiment 32
☐ 1 straw

Fig. 4-8. Blowing a bubble inside a bubble.

PROCEDURE

1 Dip the bubble horn or three-dimensional shape into the soap mix.

2 Blow into the bubble horn to make a bubble. **Do not** let the bubble leave the horn.

3 Carefully push the straw through the bubble. If you do this correctly, the bubble will not pop.

4 Slowly blow into the straw. A new bubble should appear inside.

EXPLANATION

As you saw in Experiment 33, bubbles will sometimes heal themselves after they are stuck. When you pushed the straw through the bubble, a little soap mix stuck to the end of the straw. This soap allowed you to blow another bubble.

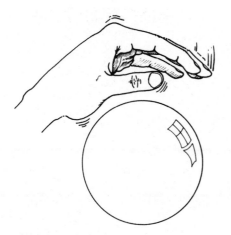

35 RACING SOAP BUBBLES

You and a friend can race your bubbles through an obstacle course.

MATERIALS

☐ soap mix (see Chapter 4 introduction)
☐ something to make large bubbles—
  string, pipe cleaners, bubble horn, plastic rings, etc.
☐ 1 pan

Fig. 4-9. Making a bubble move.

PROCEDURE

1 Pour the soap mix into the pan.
2 Dip your bubble maker into the soap and pull it through the air to release the bubble.
3 To make the bubble move, quickly move your hand back and forth. Your hand should be on the side of the bubble in the direction you want it to move. For example, to make the bubble rise, move your hand above the bubble. To make the bubble go forward, move your hand in front of the bubble.

EXPLANATION

Remember Bernouilli's Principle? (Experiments 11 through 13) Moving air pushes less than air that is not moving. By moving your hand, the air on that side pushes less. The air on the opposite side pushes more and makes the bubble move.

5
Properties of Water

Water is a wonderful chemical. It can take the shape of any container. It freezes, or becomes solid at a temperature that is not too cold. It boils, or turns to steam at a temperature that is not too hot. As water evaporates, or turns to gas, it removes much heat and makes things cooler. This is what happens when you sweat. You can add much heat to water, but the temperature will change slowly. Many different chemicals can be dissolved or mixed with water. The molecules of water stick to each other.

Because of all these traits of water, water is very important for life. Life without water would not exist. You could live many days, even weeks, without food, but you could only live 2 to 3 days without water. In this chapter, you will see some of the properties of water. You will see other properties of water in Chapter 7: Heat.

36 GUESSING HOW MUCH CONTAINERS HOLD

Your eyes sometimes trick you. You might think a glass or bowl will hold more than another one will. When you measure the containers, sometimes you find that your guess was wrong.

MATERIALS

☐ many different glasses, cups, jars, bowls, etc. Some should be tall and skinny. Others should be short and fat.
☐ water from faucet
☐ 1 large measuring cup
☐ paper and pencil

Fig. 5-1. Measuring different containers.

PROCEDURE

1 Look at all of the glasses you set out on the counter. Guess which one will hold the most water. Guess which glass will hold the least water.

2 Write down your guesses on the paper.

3 Fill each glass to the top with water.

4 Ask an adult to help you, or show you, how to use a measuring cup.

5 Pour the water from one glass into the measuring cup. Be careful not to spill any water.

6 Measure how much water the glass holds.

7 Draw the shape of the glass and write down how much water it holds.

8 Repeat steps 5 through 8 for each glass.

Were your guesses correct? Were you surprised how much or how little some glasses held.

EXPLANATION

Scientists and other people use their eyes to observe things. They seldom use only their eyes to measure, however. They usually use a tool such as a ruler or measuring cup to measure. A careful scientist always writes things down as soon as he or she does something. You might think that you can remember things, but your brain is not always that good. **Always write down what you see or measure.**

Fig. 5-2. Increased water level after adding coins.

37 "MAGICALLY" FILLING A GLASS

You can use pieces of money to make the amount of water *seem* to increase.

MATERIALS

- ☐ 1 small glass
- ☐ ¹/₂ cup (4 ounces or 120ml) water
- ☐ 10 coins or small stones
- ☐ 1 measuring cup
- ☐ 1 marking pen

PROCEDURE

1 Measure ¹/₂ cup of water.

2 Pour the water into the glass.

3 Draw a line on the glass to show the top of the water.

4 Slowly and carefully add 10 or more coins or stones to the water. Try not to let the water splash.

5 Draw a line on the glass to show the new level of water. Do you think there is now more water in the glass than when you started?

6 Carefully pour all of the water back into the measuring cup. Do not let the coins fall into the measuring cup.

7 Measure how much water is in the cup. It still should be ¹/₂ cup.

EXPLANATION

The amount of water cannot be increased unless you add more water. The reason the water level rose is that the coins or stones took up some of the water's space. The coins or stones pushed the water away. The water had no place to go except to move higher in the glass.

38 PUSHING WATER WITH DIFFERENT COINS

This experiment is similar to Experiment 37, except here you will experiment with different types of coins.

MATERIALS

- ☐ 1 small glass
- ☐ water from faucet
- ☐ two types of many coins (pennies and dimes or pennies and nickels work well)
- ☐ 1 marking pen

Fig. 5-3. Spilling water with quarters.

PROCEDURE

1 Fill the glass with water so that water is about ¹/₂ inch (1cm) from the top.

2 Draw a line on the glass at the top of the water.

3 Slowly drop one penny at a time into the glass. Keep adding pennies until the water spills over the edge.

4 Pour out the water and count how many pennies you used.

5 Fill the glass again to the same line.

6 Slowly drop nickels or dimes or quarters into the glass until the water spills over.

7 Pour out the water and count the coins.

　　Did you need the same number of coins each time?

EXPLANATION

As you saw in Experiment 37, money takes up space and pushes the water up. The amount of water pushed depends on how heavy the coin is. The heavier coin will push more water, and you will need fewer of the heavier coins.

39 MAGICAL MOVEMENT OF WATER

Pepper placed on the surface of water suddenly moves toward the edge of the bowl.

MATERIALS

☐ 1 cereal bowl filled with water
☐ white pepper
☐ 1 toothpick
☐ dish detergent

Fig. 5-4. Dipping the detergent-coated toothpick.

PROCEDURE

1 Fill the bowl with water.
2 Sprinkle pepper on the surface so that most of the surface is covered with a thin layer.
3 Dip the toothpick through the pepper. Does anything happen?
4 Now place a drop of dish detergent on the end of a toothpick.
5 Dip the toothpick into the water and watch the pepper move.

EXPLANATION

Water molecules are held together in such a way that many objects can float on the surface of water. This property is called surface tension. The dish detergent contains molecules that are greasy, and greasy molecules don't mix well with water. These greasy molecules disrupt some of the water and push the water away. You can also do this experiment with other spices. Some will work, and some will not.

Dipping the toothpick without detergent is important. Had you only used the detergent-coated toothpick, you would not know if the toothpick or the detergent made the pepper move.

40 FLOATING AND SINKING NEEDLES

You can float a needle on water, then magically make it sink.

MATERIALS

☐ 1 bowl of water
☐ 1 needle
☐ dish detergent

Fig. 5-5. Using paper to float a needle.

PROCEDURE

1 Fill the bowl with water.
2 Carefully place the needle on the surface. If you do this step correctly, the needle will float on the surface. This step requires practice and a steady hand.
3 Add a drop of dish detergent near the needle. The needle should sink.

If you cannot make the needle float, try this:

1 Place a small piece of tissue paper on the surface of the water.
2 Carefully place the needle on the paper.
3 Slowly touch a corner of the paper with a pencil. The paper should sink, and the needle should float.
4 Now add a drop of detergent.

EXPLANATION

The needle floats because of surface tension (see Experiment 39). The dish detergent breaks the bonds that are responsible for surface tension. With no surface tension, the needle sinks.

Salt

String

Fig. 5-6. Salt and string on an ice cube.

41 PICKING UP ICE WITH A STRING

Bet a friend that you can pick up an ice cube with a piece of string.

MATERIALS

☐ 1 salt shaker
☐ 1 cube of ice
☐ 1 piece of string, about 4 inches (10cm) long

PROCEDURE

1 Place the ice cube on the counter.

2 Place the string on top of the ice cube.

3 Raise the string. Does the cube move?

4 Replace the string on top of the cube.

5 Sprinkle salt on top of cube and over the string.

6 Wait 2 to 5 minutes.

7 Raise the string. Does the cube move now?

EXPLANATION

Salt makes the ice melt and then refreeze at a lower temperature. As the ice melts, the string forms a groove in the ice cube. As the water refreezes, it freezes around the string so that the string is now inside the cube.

6
General Biology

Biology is the branch of science that deals with living things. To most people, living things are plants and animals. If you did some experiments in Chapter 3, you saw that bacteria and molds were also a type of life.

Different forms of life are all around you. You can study all types of life by looking around your yard or nearby woods. This chapter has two parts. The first part contains experiments with plants. The second part contains experiments with animals. In some cases, you will be just looking, and in other cases, you will actually try different things. When you look, use your eyes carefully.

Do not kill any of the live animals you find or use. All animals have a place in the world.

42 COUNTING DIFFERENT TYPES OF PLANTS

You can find plants in many different places. The type of plant you find in a particular place will depend on how much light and water is in a given place. You will need two different areas in your yard or on your school grounds.

MATERIALS

☐ 4 pieces of string, 1 yard (1 meter) long
☐ paper and pencil

Fig. 6-1. Counting different plants.

PROCEDURE

1 Find a place that is in the sun most of the day.
2 Lay down the pieces of string to form a square as shown in Fig. 6-1.
3 Count the number of different plants you see. Use the shape of the leaves to help distinguish different plants. Some plants are very small, and you might have to get down on your knees to see these.
4 Write down the number of different plants you see.
5 Now find an area that is in the shade most of the day.
6 Repeat steps 2 to 4.
7 Draw a bar graph of your results like the one shown in Fig. 6-2.

Which area had more different types of plants? Did you see any plants that were the same in both areas?

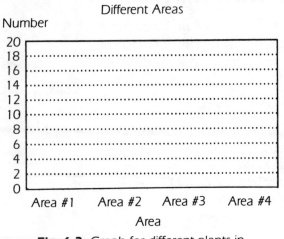

Fig. 6-2. Graph for different plants in different areas.

EXPLANATION

Different plants need different amounts of light to grow. Plants that need little light usually will not grow in direct sunlight. The soil in sunny areas is usually different from the soil in shady areas. This is why you probably saw different plants in the two areas.

43 GROWING SEEDS PART 1

In this experiment, you will be able to see what happens when you plant seeds in the ground. This experiment will take many days.

MATERIALS

☐ 1 package of bean seeds (Available in garden shops. *Don't* use beans that are sold as food in grocery stores. These beans usually will not grow.)
☐ 1 roll of paper towels
☐ 2 small plates or saucers

Fig. 6-3. Moistening a paper towel to sprout seeds.

PROCEDURE

1 Place 3 to 5 seeds on each plate.
2 Cover one plate with a dry paper towel.
3 Cover one plate with a wet paper towel.
4 Place both plates on the counter.
5 Check the wet paper towels three times a day. *If it is dry*, make it wet again, and place it back on the seeds.
6 One time each day, lift the towels and examine the seeds. Replace the towels.
7 Repeat Step 6 for 7 to 10 days.

What happened? Which seeds began to grow?

EXPLANATION

Water is necessary for seeds to start growing. Water helps the seed to form its shoots and roots. What you saw each day usually happens underground out of sight.

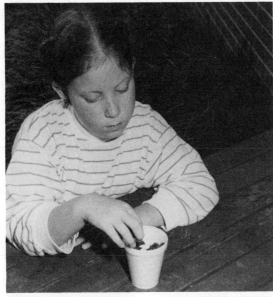

Fig. 6-4. Planting seeds.

44 GROWING SEEDS PART 2

In this experiment, you will watch a seed turn into a plant. You might want to do Experiments 43 and 44 at the same time. This experiment will take about two weeks.

MATERIALS

☐ 1 package of bean seeds (see Experiment 43)
☐ 1 styrofoam cup (or small pot)
☐ 1 tablespoon
☐ water from faucet
☐ paper and pencil
☐ colored pencils or marking pens
☐ ruler
☐ potting soil or dirt to fill the cup

PROCEDURE

1 Fill the cup or pot with dirt. Don't pack the dirt too tightly.

2 Put 3 seeds in the dirt, and cover with about ¹/₂ inch (1cm) of dirt. Space the seeds evenly around the dirt.

3 Add 3 tablespoons of water to the dirt.

4 Place the cup or pot in the window.

5 Add 3 tablespoons of water to the container each day.

6 Determine how many days it takes before you see the plant above the dirt.

7 When the seeds start to grow, measure the height in millimeters each day.

8 Write down what you measure.

9 Do steps 7 and 8 each day for 14 or more days.

10 Make a bar graph that shows the growth each day (see Fig. 6-5). Use a different color for each plant. An adult might have to help you make the graph.

Did all the seeds grow the same amount? At the same rate? When did you first see the plant?

You can do this experiment with any seeds. You can see which seeds grow the fastest. When you carve a pumpkin, try growing a pumpkin plant from the seeds. You probably won't get a pumpkin, but you will get a nice big plant. Young children can do this experiment without measuring.

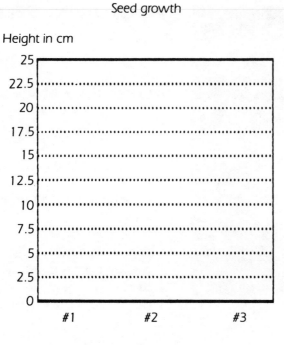

Height in cm

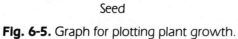

Seed

Fig. 6-5. Graph for plotting plant growth.

EXPLANATION

The seeds might be slightly different. Some seeds might take in water faster than other seeds. These seeds will grow faster. Other seeds might not develop as many roots, and might grow slower.

Fig. 6-6. Seeds planted with different kinds of liquids.

45 GROWING SEEDS WITH DIFFERENT LIQUIDS

How well do plants grow in tea, cola, etc? In this experiment, you get to try growing seeds in these liquids. This experiment takes about two or three weeks.

MATERIALS

- ☐ 10 to 20 bean seeds
- ☐ 3 to 5 styrofoam cups, or small pots
- ☐ potting soil or dirt, enough to fill all of the cups
- ☐ 1 tablespoon
- ☐ water from faucet
- ☐ bottles of cola, other soft drinks, fruit juice, milk, tea, etc.
- ☐ paper and pencil
- ☐ tape
- ☐ ruler

PROCEDURE

1 Decide which liquids you will use.

2 Fill one cup for each liquid with dirt. Don't pack the dirt too tightly.

3 Prepare labels for each liquid and tape the labels to the cups. One cup must use water.

4 Place 3 seeds in each cup and cover the seeds with about 1/2 inch (1cm) of dirt.

5 Add 3 tablespoons of the different liquids to each labeled cup.

6 Place all of cups in the window or another warm, sunny spot.

7 Each day, add 3 tablespoons of additional liquid into each cup. Do this step for 14 to 21 days.

8 At the end of the experiment, measure the height of the plant in inches (or cm) of the tallest plant in each group.

9 Decide which liquids make plants grow better and which liquids make them grow worse. Compare all of results to water.

10 Make a bar graph of your results such as the one shown in Fig. 6-7.

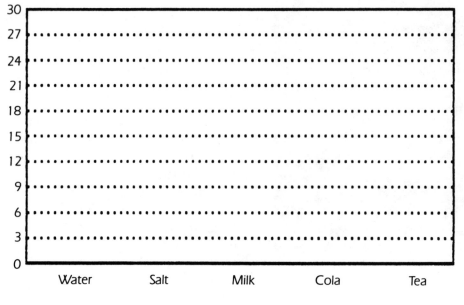

Plant growth in
different liquids

Height in cm

30
27
24
21
18
15
12
9
6
3
0

Water   Salt   Milk   Cola   Tea

Liquid

Fig. 6-7. Graph for plant growth in different liquids.

EXPLANATION

You might be surprised at your results. Most liquids that you used contain chemicals that plants cannot use. Plants get many of their chemicals from their roots. Some chemicals cannot enter the roots. Other liquids contain acids, and some acids slow down growth.

In Experiments 43 and 44, you always used more than one seed in each cup. The use of more than one seed is important. Some seeds will never grow. If you had such a seed, and if you used only one seed, you couldn't say why the seed did not grow. When you do different experiments, try to use more than one item.

Fig. 6-8. Plant on its side.

46 MAKING BENT PLANTS

The stems of plants usually grow up and down. You can make a plant with a bent stem. The experiment will take two to three weeks.

MATERIALS

☐ 1 small house plant (Coleus plants work well)

PROCEDURE

1 Place the pot with the plant on its side.
2 Place the plant in the window or in another warm, sunny spot.
3 Water the plant when the soil gets dry. To do this, you will have to turn the pot right-side up for a moment. Be sure to return the pot to its side.
4 Observe what happens to the stem. It might take two to three weeks for the stem to bend.

EXPLANATION

The top of the stem always grows up, away from the pull of gravity. When you turn the plant on its side, the stem bends so the tip will grow up.

47 BENDING PLANTS 2

In Experiment 46, you saw how to make a plant with a bent stem. This experiment uses light to produce a bent stem. The experiment will take one to two weeks.

MATERIALS

- ☐ store-bought bean seeds
- ☐ 1 cup
- ☐ soil to fill cup
- ☐ water from faucet
- ☐ 1 cardboard milk container (1 quart size) or one adult size shoe box
- ☐ aluminum foil, if you use a shoe box
- ☐ 1 tablespoon

Fig. 6-9. Carton to use in light-bending experiment.

PROCEDURE

If you grew seeds in Experiment 44, you can use those plants if they are 2 to 3 inches (5 to 8cm) high. Skip to step 3.

1 If you don't have some young plants, fill the cup with soil and plant three seeds in the dirt.

2 Add 3 tablespoons of water to the soil each day.

3 When plants are 2 to 3 inches (5 to 8cm) high, remove all but one of the plants.

4 Cut the bottom of the milk carton (about 3 inches (8cm) from the top of the carton), then cut a 1¹/₂ × 1¹/₂ inch (3 × 3 cm) square off one side of the box. See Fig. 6-9.

5 Add enough water to the cup so that the soil is moist. Eight to ten tablespoons is probably about right.

6 Place the plant on a table or in a window.

7 Cover the plant with the box.

8 Allow the plant to sit covered for many days. Do not remove the box.

9 After 5 to 10 days, the plant should appear through the hole.

10 Remove the box and examine the shape of the stem. Is it bent?

Fig. 6-10. Covering the plant.

EXPLANATION

Most plants bend toward the light. Since the light comes from the side, the stem bent to find the light.

48 THE DISAPPEARING BLOOD VESSEL

In this experiment, you can repeat a famous experiment that Sir William Harvey did over 300 years ago. He showed that blood moved only one way through the body. This experiment is best done with two people.

MATERIALS

☐ your arm

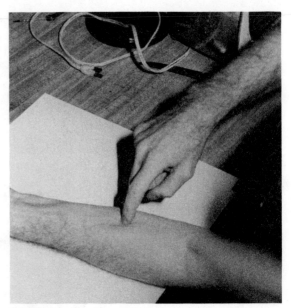

Fig. 6-11. Placing a finger on a vein in the arm.

PROCEDURE

1 Find one of the big veins in your arm. Veins appear blue and carry blood back to the heart.
2 Have your partner place a finger on one of the veins.
3 With the other hand, smooth out the vein by pushing toward the shoulders 2 to 3 times. What happens to the vein? Can you see it?
4 Release the finger. What happens to the vein?
5 Wait 2 to 3 minutes and push on the vein again.
6 Now smooth out the vein by pushing toward the wrist 2 to 3 times. Does the vein disappear this time?

EXPLANATION

Blood flows in only one direction to the heart. It flows from the wrist toward the shoulder. When you pressed the vein, you blocked the vein and prevented blood from flowing past the block.

You forced the blood through the vein toward the shoulder. No new blood could enter the vein because you had it blocked. When you pushed the blood toward the wrist, it still flowed back to the block. When William Harvey did this experiment, people did not know that blood moved through the body.

49 WHAT LIVES IN SOIL

Fig. 6-12. Examining soil for animals.

You probably have not thought about the kind of animals that live in soil. In this experiment, you will try to find animals from the soil.

MATERIALS

- ☐ soil from two different areas, such as a sunny area and a shaded area, or garden dirt and sand
- ☐ 1 small shovel
- ☐ 2 containers—jars, tin cans, tennis ball containers, etc.
- ☐ 1 to 2 sheets of newspaper
- ☐ paper and pencil

PROCEDURE

1 Pick two different areas to gather your soil. Shady and sunny areas are fine. Two different types of soil, such as sand and dirt, are even better.

2 With the shovel, fill the containers with dirt. Try to dig down 3 to 5 inches (7-12cm).

3 Pour the soil on the newspaper. Spread out the soil.

4 Look for different kinds of animals.

5 Make a list of how many different animals you see. Determine which soil had the largest number of animals? Use a chart such as the one shown in Fig. 6-13. Did you see the same kind of animals in each soil? See Fig. 6-13.

Animals in
different soils

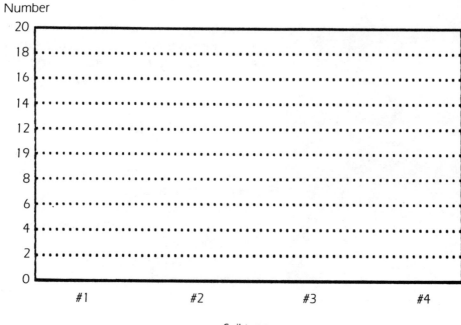

Number

20
18
16
14
12
19
8
6
4
2
0

#1   #2   #3   #4

Soil type

Fig. 6-13. Graph for animals from different areas.

EXPLANATION

Different types of soils provide different types of food. Some animals might live in one place but not in another.

Fig. 6-14. Examining a bird's nest.

50 HOW BIRDS MAKE BIRD NESTS

If you have never looked at a bird's nest, you might be surprised at what you might see.

MATERIALS

☐ 1 *empty* bird nest
☐ paper and pencil

PROCEDURE

1 Find an empty bird nest.
2 Look at the nest carefully.
3 Make a list of the different materials that are in the nest. You might be surprised at some of the materials.
4 Try to figure out how the nest was made. Was the material woven like a basket? Was it just piled together?

EXPLANATION

Different birds build nests in different ways. The way the nest is made can often tell you what kind of bird built the nest. Try to find other nest to look at.

51 THE FABULOUS SPIDER WEB

The spider web is a wonderful "building" made by an animal. The more you look at a spider web, the more you will discover.

MATERIALS

☐ 1 spider web (Even better is a spider building the web.)

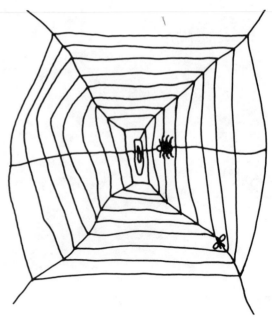

Fig. 6-15. Spider in a spider web.

PROCEDURE

1 If you are lucky enough to discover a spider building a web, watch closely. The process of making a web is fascinating.

2 If a spider is in the web, touch part of the web with a blade of grass or a stick. What does the spider do?

3 Watch the spider when an insect gets caught in the web. What does the spider do?

4 If no spider is in the web, take a piece of the web. Pull it. Notice how strong the "string" is.

Spiders are helpful animals. They help to reduce the number of insects. But spiders can be dangerous, even to people. A spider injects a poison into a fly to kill or to slow down the fly. Sometimes, a spider will bite a human. The bitten area might swell up. A few spiders, like the Brown Recluse Spider, can make people very sick when they bite.

Spiders usually make a web in a particular way. They use different types of silk for different parts of the web. Touching the web makes the silk vibrate. Spiders detect the vibration, and move toward the vibrating area.

52 ANIMALS IN A PINE CONE

Fig. 6-16. Pine cone in a funnel.

Did you know that many animals often live in a pine cone? In this experiment, you will see what kinds of animals can be found in a pine cone. This experiment takes 7 to 10 days.

MATERIALS

- [ ] 1 large kitchen funnel
- [ ] 1 large, wide-mouth jar (A large mayonnaise jar or large coffee can)
- [ ] 1 small jar (a baby food jar or small jar for olives)
- [ ] ¹/₂ cup rubbing alcohol
- [ ] 1 25-watt light bulb
- [ ] 1 lamp with flexible arm, such as "clip-on" bed light
- [ ] paper towel or sheet or paper
- [ ] tweezers (forceps)
- [ ] magnifying glass (optional)
- [ ] 2 to 4 pine cones
- [ ] kitchen tongs

PROCEDURE

1. Fill the small jar half full with the alcohol. **DO NOT TASTE THE ALCOHOL. SET IT OUT OF REACH WHEN YOU'RE DONE.**
2. Use the tongs or tweezers to place the small jar in the large jar.
3. Place the funnel in the large jar. The edge of the funnel should stick over the edge of the jar.
4. Place the pine cones in the funnel.
5. Place the light 2 to 4 inches (5 to 10cm) above the pine cones. See Fig. 6-16.
6. Turn on the light and leave the light on for 5 to 7 days.
7. After 5 to 7 days, turn off the light and remove the funnel.
8. Remove the small jar.
9. With tweezers, remove the animals to the paper and look at them. If you have a magnifying glass, you might want to use it.

EXPLANATION

The light heats up the pine cones. The animals move away from the heat and fall into the alcohol. The alcohol kills them. If you want to collect live animals, use a small jar without alcohol. You might want to repeat this experiment with a different type of pine cone—you might find different animals.

Fig. 6-17. Goldfish in a bowl.

53 HOW FAST DOES A GOLDFISH BREATHE?

Please Get Your Parent's Permission Before You Do this Experiment

If you have a goldfish, you can watch how fast its gills move. This experiment works better in the summer.

MATERIALS

- ☐ 1 goldfish
- ☐ 1 net
- ☐ 2 small goldfish bowls or large jars
- ☐ water from faucet
- ☐ clock or watch

PROCEDURE

1 Fill the 2 goldfish bowls with water.

2 Place one bowl in the refrigerator for 30 to 60 minutes.

3 Place the other bowl outside in the sun for 30 to 60 minutes.

4 Remove the bowl from the refrigerator and place it on the counter.

5 Place the goldfish in bowl.

6 Observe the movement of the gills. Count how many times they move in two minutes.

7 Carry the bowl outside and transfer the fish to the bowl of warm water using the net.

8 Watch the movement of the gills and count how many times they move in two minutes.

9 Return the fish to its original bowl.

EXPLANATION

Fish use their gills to get oxygen. There is less oxygen available in warm water than there is in cold water. In order to get the same amount of oxygen, the fish must breathe faster. When the water in lakes get too warm, many fish die because they cannot get enough oxygen.

7

Properties of Heat

From the time you were very young, you could tell the difference between hot and cold. Heat is a form of energy and always moves from a hot area to a cooler area. Different materials gain heat at different rates. Heat makes many things happen more quickly. Air that is warm tends to rise. In this chapter, you will see how fast things heat or cool and how heat changes the speed of reactions.

54 HOLDING A HOT EGG

Adult Supervision Required

Show your friend that you, but not he or she, can hold a hot cooked egg.

MATERIALS

☐ 1 egg
☐ 1 pan of water
☐ water from the faucet

Fig. 7-1. Passing a hot egg from person to person.

PROCEDURE

1 Place the egg in the pan of water.
2 Heat the pan on the stove. Let the water boil 15 to 20 minutes. Have an adult help you do this.
3 Pour out the hot water.
4 Fill the pan with cold water.
5 Let the egg sit in the cold water about 10 seconds.
6 Remove the egg and hold it in your hand for 10 to 20 seconds.
7 Give the egg to someone else. It will probably be too hot for him to hold.

EXPLANATION

Different items hold heat longer than others. The cold water cooled the shell but not the inside of the egg. After a while, some of the heat inside was transferred back to the shell. Heat always moves from areas with lots of heat to areas of low heat.

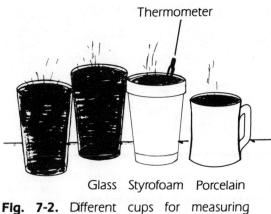

Thermometer

Glass   Styrofoam   Porcelain

Fig. 7-2. Different cups for measuring temperature change.

55 TESTING INSULATED CONTAINERS

In this experiment you can determine which type of container is best for keeping liquids warm or cold.

MATERIALS

- ☐ 1 styrofoam cup
- ☐ 1 drinking glass
- ☐ 1 pottery or porcelain coffee mug
- ☐ 1 plastic cup
- ☐ 1 empty tin can with one end removed or 1 empty soft drink can
- ☐ other insulators like a foam sleeve for a glass
- ☐ 1 thermometer from 40° to 200° F (4 to 90° C)—available in hardware and cooking stores. A thermometer for a fish tank also works.
- ☐ 1 measuring cup
- ☐ water from faucet
- ☐ paper and pencil
- ☐ clock

PROCEDURE

1 Turn on the hot water and let it run for 2 to 3 minutes.

2 With a measuring cup, put the same amount of hot water into each container.

3 Measure the temperature in each container with the thermometer. Write down the temperatures.

4 Wait five minutes, and measure the temperatures again. Write down the temperatures.

5 Measure the temperatures 10 minutes and 15 minutes after you first added the water. Write down the temperatures.

6 Prepare a graph of your measurements such as the one shown in Fig. 7-3.

Which container made the water cool fastest? Which container made the water cool the slowest?

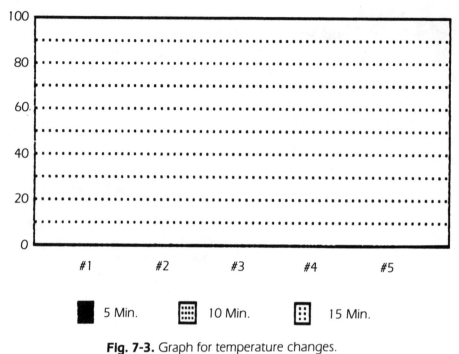

Temperature
Changes

Temperature

Fig. 7-3. Graph for temperature changes.

EXPLANATION

Heat always moves from a hot area to a cold area. Different materials cause the heat to move at different speeds. You might want to try this experiment again using cold water instead of hot water. In this case, the water will get warmer. Try as many different containers as you can.

Fig. 7-4. Measuring temperatures.

56 TESTING SOIL TEMPERATURES

In this experiment you will see how fast different soils and other items heat up. You should do this experiment on a hot, sunny day.

MATERIALS

- ☐ 3 to 6 cups, all of the same size and material
- ☐ water from faucet
- ☐ sand
- ☐ dirt
- ☐ stones
- ☐ other items such as grass clippings
- ☐ thermometer (see Experiment 55)
- ☐ paper and pencil

PROCEDURE

1 Fill one cup with water. Allow the water to warm to air temperature.

2 Fill one cup with dirt.

3 Fill one cup with sand.

4 Fill one cup with stones.

5 Measure the temperature of the material in each cup, and write it down.

6 Place all of the cups outside in a sunny area.

7 Wait 30 to 60 minutes.

8 Measure the temperature of each cup, and write them down.

Which cup heated up most? Which cup heated least.

EXPLANATION

Water can absorb much heat without much change in temperature. Soil and stones heat up much faster. For this reason, water is a good insulator. In the summer, the air over land is usually warmer than air over water. The cooler air settles under the warm air and the warm air rises making a breeze that comes from the water. At night, the land cools more quickly than the water, and a breeze blows toward the water.

57 OBSERVING RISING HEAT

You can demonstrate that warm air and warm water will rise.

MATERIALS

☐ 1 large wide-mouth jar
☐ 1 small baby food jar
☐ 2 to 3 drops of food coloring
☐ hot and cold water from a faucet
☐ 1 piece of string, 8 to 12 inches (20 to 30cm) long

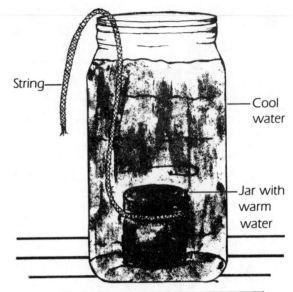

String

Cool water

Jar with warm water

Fig. 7-5. Placing warm, colored water in cool water.

PROCEDURE

1 Tie the string around the baby food jar.
2 Fill the big jar with cold water.
3 Fill the small jar with hot water.
4 Place 2 to 3 drops of food coloring in the small jar. Mix the coloring so that the water is all one color.
5 Carefully lower the small jar into the big jar.
6 Watch what happens to the colored hot water.

EXPLANATION

Heat tends to rise. You saw the hot, colored water rise in the cold water. You might want to try this again, but this time put cold water in the small jar and hot water in the large jar.

Fig. 7-6. Placing baking powder into water.

58 TIMING THE FIZZ

In this experiment, you will see what temperature makes bubbles form faster.

MATERIALS

- ☐ ¹/₂ cup of warm or hot water
- ☐ ¹/₂ cup of cold water
- ☐ 2 cups, glasses, or jars
- ☐ 2 teaspoons of baking powder (not baking soda)

PROCEDURE

1 Fill one container with ¹/₂ cup of warm or hot water.

2 Fill the other cup with ¹/₂ cup of cold water.

3 Fill 2 teaspoons half-full with baking powder.

4 At the same time, dump baking powder into each cup.

5 Watch how fast and how many bubbles form in each cup.

EXPLANATION

Heat speeds up most chemical reactions. Some of the chemicals in baking powder react with water to form carbon dioxide, the bubbles you saw. The reaction was faster in hot water.

The same thing happens when you place Alka Seltzer tablets in water. Baking powder and Alka Seltzer contain some of the same chemicals.

8

Properties of Light

The light we see is really made up of many different colors of light. These colors can be separated or combined. Light cannot pass through all objects. Light travels in straight lines. We see things because light bounces off (reflects) objects and enters our eyes. In this chapter, you'll learn how light can play tricks with your eyes.

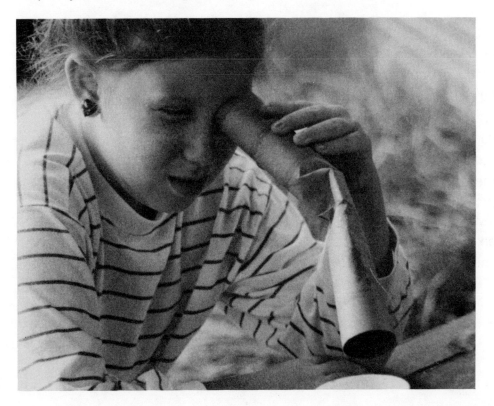

59 A HOMEMADE PRISM

When light passes through glass or water, the colors of the rainbow appear. A prism is a device that splits white light into many different colors. In this experiment, you can make your own prism. This experiment requires about 10 hours.

MATERIALS

- ☐ 1 package of unflavored gelatin
- ☐ knife
- ☐ glass measuring cup
- ☐ bread pan
- ☐ water from faucet
- ☐ pan
- ☐ hot plate or stove
- ☐ flashlight

Fig. 8-1. Using a homemade prism.

PROCEDURE

1 Heat some water on the stove until it boils. Please let an adult help you.

2 Pour the gelatin into the measuring cup.

3 Fill the cup with 1 cup of boiling water. Stir the water to dissolve the gelatin.

4 Pour the dissolved gelatin into a bread pan.

5 Add 2 to 3 cups of cold water to the pan.

6 Place the pan in the refrigerator for about 10 hours, or overnight.

7 When the gelatin is solid, remove the pan from the refrigerator.

8 Ask an adult to remove the gelatin, and cut out a shape such as the one shown in Fig. 8-2. The gelatin will stay solid for 10 to 20 minutes.

9 Darken the room.

10 Shine the flashlight on the gelatin prism and see what colors appear.

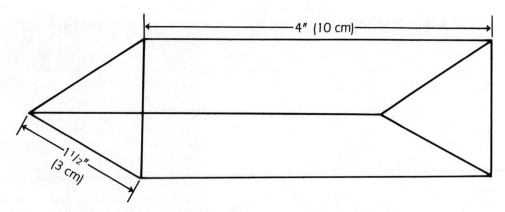

Fig. 8-2. What the prism should look like.

EXPLANATION

Light traveling through glass slows down and is bent. Different colors are bent at different angles. The result is many different colors, as in a rainbow.

The same thing happens when a rainbow is formed. Sunlight is bent as it passes through drops of rain, and different colors appear.

60 MEASURING SHADOWS

The shadow your body makes changes at different times of the day. This experiment goes on all day.

MATERIALS

- ☐ many pieces of paper or string
- ☐ many rocks, small pieces of wood, or other heavy objects
- ☐ pencil
- ☐ chalk (optional)

Fig. 8-3. Measuring a shadow.

PROCEDURE

1 Go outside and place a sheet of paper on the ground. Place weights on the paper so that it won't blow away. Or, you can stand on the sidewalk and mark where you are standing with chalk.

2 Ask a friend or an adult to mark where the head of your shadow is. Write the time on the paper or sidewalk.

3 Two to three hours later, go outside again and stand in the same place.

4 Mark the position of the head of your shadow.

5 Repeat steps 3 and 4 one or two more times during the day. Did your shadow stay in the same place? Was it the same size?

EXPLANATION

A shadow forms because light does not pass through your body. The earth spins so that the position of the sun changes throughout the day. Shadows will be shorter when the light is almost overhead.

You can do a similar experiment inside with a can and a flashlight. Move the flashlight to different places, and look at the shadow.

Fig. 8-4. Looking straight at an object.

61 LOOKING AROUND CORNERS

In this experiment you will try to view an object around a corner.

MATERIALS

- ☐ 2 shoe boxes or similar boxes or 1 tube from an empty roll of paper towels
- ☐ 1 small toy
- ☐ 1 small mirror
- ☐ scissors

PROCEDURE

1 Cut a hole on each end of one shoe box. Make sure the holes are the same height.
2 On the other shoe box, cut a hole on one end, and a hole on one side.
3 Place a toy a few inches (cm) from the hole on the first box.
4 Look through the other hole. Do you see the toy?
5 Now place the toy a few inches from one hole of the second box.
6 Look through the other hole. Do you see the toy now?
7 If you have a small mirror, place it in the second box. Move the mirror until you can see the toy.

Alternate procedure if you have no boxes:

1 Look at a toy through a paper towel tube.
2 Now bend the tube and look again. Can you see the toy now?

Fig. 8-5. Looking at an object through a bent tube.

EXPLANATION

Light travels in a straight line. In order for you to see around a corner, you must use a mirror to reflect or bend the light. Mirrors are used in headlights of cars. The light hits the mirror and is bent in different directions.

Fig. 8-6. Spinning a three-colored disk.

62 CHANGING COLOR PATTERNS

When you spin a disk with different colors, white, or new colors, appear.

MATERIALS

- ☐ 1 3 to 5 inch (7 to 12cm) circle cut from poster board
- ☐ 1 thumbtack
- ☐ red, green, and blue crayons or markers
- ☐ 1 pencil with an eraser
- ☐ 1 electric drill with a drill bit (optional)

PROCEDURE

1 Divide the circle into three equal sections.

2 Color one area red, one green, and one blue.

3 Push the thumbtack through the center of the circle.

4 Attach the circle to the eraser on the pencil. The circle must be able to spin freely.

5 Spin the circle as fast as you can. What colors do you see?

If you do not see white, the circle might not be spinning fast enough.

1 With the help of an adult, attach the circle to a drill bit in an electric drill.

2 Turn on the drill for a few seconds.

3 Observe the color.

Do not do this without an adult's help.

EXPLANATION

White is a mixture of all colors. As the circle spins, the colors seem to blend together to make white. You can try combinations of other colors on other circles to see what color appears.

63 CHANGING COLOR PATTERNS—2

This experiment is similar to Experiment 62, except the circle is black and white.

MATERIALS

- ☐ 2 or more 3 to 5 inch (7 to 12cm) circles cut from poster board
- ☐ 1 thumbtack
- ☐ black crayon or marking pen
- ☐ 1 pencil with an eraser
- ☐ 1 electrical drill (optional)

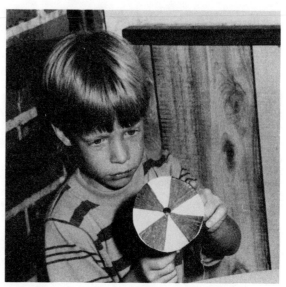

Fig. 8-7. Spinning a black and white disk.

PROCEDURE

1 Color the circle with the black marker or pen to match one of the patterns shown in Fig. 8-8.

2 Place the thumbtack through the center of the circle.

3 Attach the thumbtack to the eraser or attach the circle to an electrical drill (see Experiment 62).

4 Spin the circle.

5 Observe the color or pattern you see.

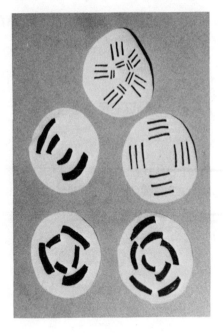

Fig. 8-8. Different patterns of disks.

EXPLANATION

As the circle spins, your eye sees different colors. Try as many patterns as you can, and make your own patterns.

64 THE REVERSIBLE ARROW

An arrow drawn on paper magically changes direction.

MATERIALS

- ☐ 1 index card or piece of paper
- ☐ 1 pen or marking pen
- ☐ 1 clean glass or jar
- ☐ water from the faucet

Fig. 8-9. Looking at an arrow through a glass.

PROCEDURE

1 Draw an arrow on the paper. The arrow should be about 2 inches (5cm) long.

2 Fill a glass with water.

3 Place the paper behind the glass and slowly move the paper away from you.

4 Watch the arrow through the glass. What happens?

EXPLANATION

Light is bent by the glass and the water. When the arrow is close to the glass, the light rays from the ends cross before they reach your eyes. The arrow appears reversed. When the arrow is far from the glass, the rays do not cross, and the arrow appears as it is on the card.

Lenses in microscopes and magnifying glasses bend the light rays so that things appear larger.

9
Properties of Magnets

Magnets usually pick up items that have iron in them. All magnets have two ends, or poles, a North pole and a South pole. The opposite ends of the two magnets attract each other. Like ends of magnets repel, or push away each other. Magnets can be damaged by dropping them.

Magnets are fun to play with, but they are also very useful. Some magnets are used to make electricity. Other magnets can be found in telephones and doorbells. The experiments in this chapter can all be done with a small, refrigerator magnet. If you don't have a magnet, you can buy a magnetic strip in a craft store.

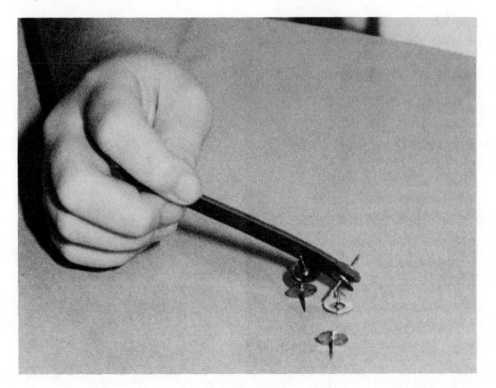

65 TESTING FOR IRON

In this experiment, you will test many items to see if they contain iron. Items that contain iron will stick to a magnet.

MATERIALS

- ☐ 1 magnet
- ☐ many different items: silverware, pens, different pans, etc.
- ☐ paper and pencil

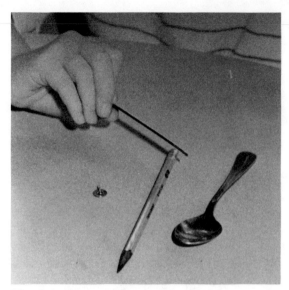

Fig. 9-1. Testing different items for iron.

PROCEDURE

CAUTION: NEVER PUT A MAGNET NEAR A COMPUTER, A COMPUTER DISK, A VCR OR TELEVISION. A MAGNET WILL DAMAGE THESE ITEMS.

1 Touch the magnet to the stove. Does it stick to the stove?
2 Test a piece of silverware to see if a magnet will stick.
3 Try many other items to see if they will stick to the magnet.
4 Make a list of all things that a magnet sticks to and a list of things it will not stick to.

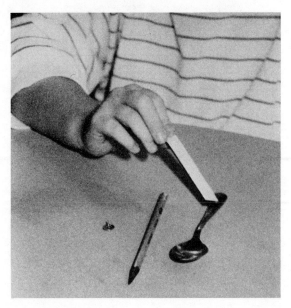

Fig. 9-2. Testing different items for iron.

EXPLANATION

A magnet usually sticks to anything that contains iron. Some metals, such as steel, contain iron. Other metals, such as aluminum foil, do not contain iron.

66 HOW STRONG IS A MAGNET?

Try to see how many things a magnet will pick up at one time.

MATERIALS

☐ 1 magnet
☐ many thumbtacks, pins, paper clips, etc.

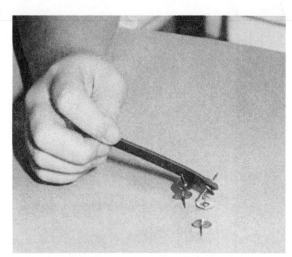

Fig. 9-3. Picking up many tacks with a magnet.

PROCEDURE

1 Spread out the items you will try to pick up with the magnet.
2 Touch the magnet to one item.
3 Now touch the first item to another item. Is it picked up?
4 Try to pick up as many items as you can. If you have more than one magnet, try to see which magnet is stronger.

EXPLANATION

A magnet exerts its effect through another object. The second object behaves temporarily like a magnet.

10

Other Experiments

The two experiments in this section don't fall into any special category, but they are fun to do. You will learn how to make large amounts of foam and how to make your own paper.

67 MAKING YOUR OWN FOAM

When you pour a soft drink such as cola into a glass, foam forms at the top. You can make lots of your own foam by mixing vinegar and baking soda.

MATERIALS

- ☐ 1 measuring cup
- ☐ 1 tall drinking glass
- ☐ 1 box baking soda
- ☐ 1 bottle of vinegar
- ☐ 1 teaspoon
- ☐ water from the faucet

Fig. 10-1. Pouring baking soda into vinegar.

PROCEDURE

CAUTION: WHEN DOING THIS EXPERIMENT, KEEP YOUR FACE AWAY FROM THE DRINKING GLASS. THE VINEGAR MIGHT SPLATTER INTO YOUR EYES.

1 Place 1 to 2 teaspoons of baking soda in the glass.

2 Measure 2 to 3 ounces (50 to 80ml) of vinegar.

3 Pour the vinegar into the glass.

4 Observe how high the foam goes.

5 Rinse out the glass and repeat steps 1 through 4, but use different amounts of either vinegar or baking soda.

6 Observe how high the foam goes.

7 Rinse out the glass again, and add 1 to 2 teaspoons of baking soda.

8 Measure 2 to 3 ounces (50 to 80ml) of water.

9 Pour the water into the glass. Did the foam form? If so, how much?

Fig. 10-2. Foam in a glass.

EXPLANATION

The chemicals in vinegar and baking soda react to form a large amount of carbon dioxide, the same gas that makes bubbles in soft drinks. You used this idea to measure the change of apple juice to vinegar in Experiment 28.

Years ago, this reaction was used to make water toys. The chemicals were placed in two compartments in a boat. The vinegar and baking soda slowly mixed, and the gas escaped and pushed the boat.

You might want to try making a similar toy with a balloon and a soft drink bottle. The baking soda should go into the balloon. Try to figure out what else you need to do. If you do it correctly, the balloon will sail off the bottle.

68 MAKING PAPER

Adult Supervision Required

You can use many different materials to make your own paper. Sawdust, old newspaper, or ground leaves are just a few examples.

MATERIALS

- [ ] paper (cut into ¹/₂ inch (1cm) strips), newspaper, or the edges torn from computer paper is fine
- [ ] 2 to 3 cups of sawdust, crumbled leaves, or shredded tissues
- [ ] water from the faucet
- [ ] 1 large pan
- [ ] blender
- [ ] 1 large dish pan or baking dish
- [ ] 1 piece of screen, any size, but 4 × 6 inches (10cm × 15cm) works well

Fig. 10-3. Dipping a screen into paper slurry.

PROCEDURE

1 Soak 3 to 5 handfuls of the paper in water for 10 to 12 minutes.

2 If you use newspaper, boil the newspaper for 10 to 20 minutes. Have an adult help you do this.

3 Place 2 to 3 large handfuls of paper into the blender. If you use sawdust, use 2 to 3 cups.

4 Add about 1 quart (1 liter) of water to blender (see Fig. 10-4).

5 Blend this mix at high speed for 20 to 30 seconds. Please have an adult help you with this.

6 Pour this blended mix into a dish pan or baking dish.

7 Hold the edges of the screen and dip the screen into the blended mix.

8 Pull the screen out of the mix and allow the water to drip out (see Fig. 10-5).

You want the mix to cover the screen, but you don't want it too thick. You might have to dip the screen a few times to get the thickness you want.

9 Place the screen in a 200°F (90°C to 92°C) for about 1¹/₂ hours until paper is dry. Be sure you have an adult's permission.

Fig. 10-4. Shredded paper in a blender.

Fig. 10-5. Homemade paper on the screen.

10 Remove the screen from the oven. Be sure to use pot holders so you don't burn yourself. Also, remember to turn off the stove.

11 Allow the screen to cool 5 to 10 minutes.

12 Peel the paper off of the screen. The edges will be jagged.

If you want straight edges, trim the sides with scissors.

This experiment allows you to recycle materials you would usually throw out. The paper you make will be thicker than most paper and gray to tan in color. You can try making colored paper if you want. To do this, add a few blueberries or strawberries or a few drops of food coloring to the blender before blending. Then proceed as directed above. Homemade paper makes great cards for holiday seasons.

Index